# Sweet and Savory

# Union

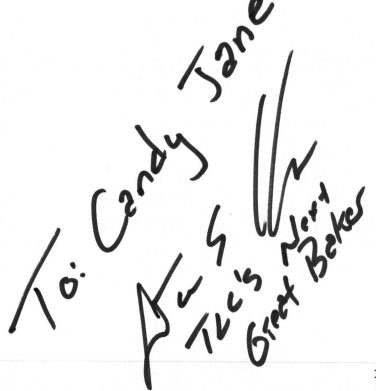

To: Candy Jane

TLC's Next
Great Baker

Desserts By Dana LLC.
22 Peterson Place
Bear, DE 19701
www.dessertsbydana.com

First Edition

All materials provided in this book by Dana Herbert are owned by Desserts By Dana LLC.

Food Photography by Dana Herbert, Desserts By Dana, LLC
Cover Photography by Derrick Smith, Nocturnal Theory Design   nocturnaltheory.com
Cover Design by Wali Barrett, WMB Designs   wmbdesigns.carbonmade.com
Wine Pairing Consultation by L. Denise Jackson   thesippingsommelier.blogspot.com

I dedicate this book to my mother for always believing in me and assuring me that the Lord always had me in his favor. She always said to him that believeth all things are possible. Thank you for being that living testimony and reminder that he is in control of everything. Thank you for the inspiration to keep moving when all seemed dim and reminding me to give thanks when things were plentiful. I love you mom. This one is for you.

And to my dad, thank you for instilling me with an unquenchable drive to Achieve. You cannot get but so mad when you see me push as hard as I do. I learned it by watching you. As they say the Apple does not fall far from the tree. Thanks for teaching me to be a man and to do what's right. There are so many bad things out there in the world but you always educated us well to make smart decisions and analyze the situation.

# Thank You from the SUGAR DADDY!!

**Thank you first and foremost to my Lord and Savior** for blessing me with the gift to be able to create food and desserts that people love. It is truly His hands that are sculpting, preparing, and seasoning everything I do. For that I am grateful that He chose me.

**Thank you to my wife** for enduring the journey to getting to where we are today. No one ever said it would be easy, but when you put God first and the house is full of love then all things are possible.

**To my mother**, I think you understand me best. I guess you should since I came from your womb (smile). You always taught me through Christ that all things are possible. You told me to never give up on my dream and to keep fighting for it. One day it shall come to pass. For all the talks and support, I truly thank you.

**To my dad**, I want to say thank you for instilling the drive to succeed. As an adolescent and young man I watched your career flourish and saw how you pushed to get to the top. So, like father like son, I have that similar mind frame. Sometimes I know you tell me to slow down but hey I get it from you!

**To my Grandmother, Aunt Queenie, Aunt Barbara, Aunt Tene, and Aunt Alverta**, thank you for keeping my taste buds happy happy happy. The house was truly filled with love and full tummies. Grand mommy you still have to teach me how to make that apple jelly and those sugar cookies.

**To my Grandfather, Uncle Peyton, Uncle Butch, Uncle Jimmy, and Uncle Richard**, thanks for always supporting and encouraging me by being great role models.

**To my cousins**, thank you for being my cake delivering and chocolate strawberry dipping divas that you are. Your efforts are greatly appreciated. Did you ever think you would be dipping strawberries until 5AM? You are pros at it now!

**To my fraternity brothers of Kappa Alpha Psi**, we have been through some things and one thing is for sure we were taught how to ACHIEVE. Robert we are going to make it! So to my NUPES Robert, E-Class, Jay, Marlon, Ced, Pimp, Eric, Wali B., Jerome, Donald, Thomas, Darnell, John Polk, Lambda Xi, Nu Xi, Xi Gamma Rutgers, Wilmington Alumni, Age, Omar, Kendall, Lil Mike, and beyond, keep pushing to those golden shores of Phi Nu Pi. "IF".

**To my friends and extended family**: Tyler and Jenny, Bobby, Kendelynn, Joan, Tara, Ron and Allyson, DJ Amaze; Spanky; Effie; Denika and Derrick; Mr. Dennis and Miss Vicky; Skee; Ivan and Treese; Redcross; Danielle; Richard Kelley and the Philadelphia Airport Marriott family, and the Philadelphia Downtown Marriott family; thank you so much. To the Pastry Puffs (Debbie, Emong, Gumer, James, Manu, Mohammed, Stephanie, and Sam), all I can say is "who made you ....huh." (smile) Delaware stand up – we did it!

**Thank you to my University of Delaware and Johnson and Wales Instructors:** Joe Digregorio; Debbie Ellingsworth; Francis Kwanza; Bob Nelson; Ron Cole; Paul Wise; Pam Cummings; Donna Laws; Dean Lavornia; David Ricci; Rainer Hienerwadel; John Aukstolis; Ciril Hitz and others. You never know how that brief time you spend with your students will inspire them to great things. Thank you for doing what you do on a daily basis.

**To my new sister Yadi**, thanks for keeping the Desserts By Dana name alive in New York. To Yomi and Jaden (Jay-Skee), we keep making the hits.

**To Cousin Lisa**, thank you for helping me with the book and continually getting on me until we got this thing done.

**Thank you to the Desserts By Dana crew**: Anik; Sinta; Vanessa; Jessica; Rachel; Tracy; Robert; and Katie. The best is yet to come.

**Last but not least by any means to my Brother Jeffrey**, Thanks for always hanging in there and sticking with me. We have grown together as kids, adolescents, and into men. Thank you for always being the best brother you could always be. I couldn't have asked for anything more from you.

# I Used to Love Her

I look back at this culinary journey and it is just mind boggling to me. When did I fall in love with her? Was it the days at grandma's counter watching her make cookies and sneaking little bits and scraps of cookie dough to eat? Was it watching my mom make that stuffed flank steak? Possibly those dinners my close friends and I had during my high school years when we really thought we knew what we were doing in the kitchen? Or maybe was it in my foods class in high school that sealed the deal? One thing is for sure, I fell hard for my first love...cooking.

Cooking is so much to love like a woman. If prepared properly and handled with care, the result is splendid, however, if not, it will leave the worst taste in your mouth and you will never forget it.

Cooking began purely as a means of survival, to feed the family. Over time it evolved into a way to fellowship, celebrate, soothe, and even a lifestyle. Cooking became more wholesome. It's a versatile and creative art: savvy and sassy, understated and satisfying, or mellow and smooth with a little bit, (or a lot) of pizzazz and spice. One thing is for sure cooking has always been the one thing that brought the family together. The laughter, and love around the table was automatic.

Food and love through my family's generations brings back so many wonderful memories. Time sort of stopped when dinner came. You just knew that's where you needed to be at that certain time every day. I am honored you have chosen this book to share with and spread through your generations at the table. To understand my cooking passion I must share with my journey what influenced my style and this book.

I always grew up in a household full of love. We were always surrounded by family on both my parent's sides so when I say I had family.... I had family. My fondest cooking memories started as a young child at my paternal grandmother's home. She made some of the best sugar cookies, jams, jellies, potato salad, and crab cakes ever. She can burn baby! She had that down home swagger to her cooking. Unfortunately, I never had the pleasure of meeting my maternal grandmother but from my mother's cooking, I could only imagine the fresh bread she made at every meal that my mother talked about often. My mom has a mixed style. She is from the country so we had everything from birch beer, and sun tea, to canned vegetables and homemade desserts you could eat until you were sick. My mother also likes to try out new recipes, so we would get the best of both worlds.

As I matured and entered high school, I was always thinking that I would be a corporate business man like my father. He was doing well for himself and became quite successful. Well, in high school I took this foods class with Linda Lakey and thought it was pretty cool. All the memories and good times centered on cooking rushed back to me and I loved it. The years went on and while in my senior year I was introduced to Hotel, Restaurant and Institutional Management. This was a great blend of business and food that I needed. I was excited and at that point tried all the baking recipes I could get my hands on. Our kitchen was full of stuff I baked. My mother had to slow me down because I was making it faster than my family could eat it all. I just wanted to see how things turned out. I was a mad scientist for a minute.

When I went off to college, I excelled in anything food related. I worked as a Student Sous Chef at Vita Nova for Joe DiGregorio, who was an excellent mentor and allowed me to do what I loved. I learned a lot from him. From the proper techniques of sautéing, grilling, as well as making oven dried tomatoes, we were doing it at Vita Nova. There were plenty of jobs outside of Vita Nova including, burger joints, nursing homes, pizza kitchens, fine dining hotels and elite country clubs. I kept my hands in everything. At one time, I had three jobs and was going to school fulltime. It was not long before my college classmates knew me as that dude that could put it down in the kitchen. I remember flipping the family room in my college apartment to a dining room with (table cloths and all) and making meals for people. Cooking was my passion and the more I loved her the more she loved me back. She has stayed with me through the years and has grown with me and I worked hard to perfect all I could for and with her. I cannot get enough of her.

Now, though I enjoyed all of those other places, Vita Nova was the place that confirmed everything I was thinking. I needed to go to Culinary School. I decided to go to the Culinary School at Johnson and Wales University. All of the dots I felt were missing before were finally connected. I loved it so much that I stayed to complete studies for pastry arts as well. When I finished, I felt complete in the sense of having a very broad set of skills. Not every chef can perform well in one area of culinary one day and excel well the next day in pastry arts. While at Johnson and Wales University, I worked at some very elite hotels, high-end bistros, and even as a Pastry Chef for a country club. I experienced so many styles of cooking from American, French, Asian, Italian, German and so much more. When I left college I felt as if I was ready to take on the world. Or so I thought.

The world opened up and I worked for Marriott and immediately was schooled to the real world, fast- paced, never say die mentality of our cooking world. I thought I was good, but they made me better. I thought I was fast, but they made me faster. I would come home exhausted sometimes, I mean rocked, but with a smile on my face because I knew I was getting better and better. Simultaneously I started my own company, Desserts By Dana (www.dessertsbydana.com). At Desserts By Dana we do everything from plated desserts to wedding and specialty cakes, as well as sugar sculptures. After a while, I transferred to the Philadelphia Downtown Marriott and then I blossomed. After all the fine dining, catering, burger restaurants, and nursing home experience I had under my belt, this was the place for me. I worked at a large convention center property. It was nothing to pump out a few thousand for breakfast, lunch, and dinner. Sixty hours a week could be a regular for us. I recall doing 95 hours one week. It was "Whatever it takes." I was no longer on the culinary side but smack dab in the middle of a high volume pastry kitchen. I loved it. I got to do more and see more in that time than I did in all my years combined. I used my skills almost to their potential. There was an executive chef there that was not always so flattering but he was honest, which I could only appreciate. He challenged us to be better, be memorable, take what the customer wants and exceed that. It was he that got me into sugar art and sculptures. Once he showed me some sugar sculptures online, I was hooked. I fell in love with her all over again. It's funny how you can love something and regardless of how she changed and evolved still loved her as much as the first time.

It is like seeing a woman for years and then all of a sudden, there is a new hair style, outfit, attitude or a few lost pounds...a new swagger is added and wow, it starts all over again. You get a chance to discover, be mesmerized, and learn her new aspect all over again.

Now here I am at a new place in this culinary journey spreading my wings and letting her take me to the next level of love. From Chaine Dinners, National Culinary Conventions, High Society Weddings, and TV shows. We did it! Together. I was fortunate to travel all over the country and try different cuisines, work with different chefs and push towards a new plateau. I began to play with all this sweet and savory stuff. Sweet and Savory is like Yin and Yang. Everything is in balance, caramel with salt or tossed salads with chocolate dressings. She and I developed our own thing. This was the beginning of my "Sweet and Savory Union."


Bon Appétit

## getting the most from sweet and savory...

Do understand that while these recipes have been specially selected for the Sweet and Savory readers, we are sensitive to allergies and ingredients that may not agree with you. Substitute an ingredient that is close with the full understanding that this may change the intended flavors, however, you may create a new gem for yourself.

### dana's faves

Under select recipe titles, there will be a notation of the chef's favorites and what the occasion they may be a favorite to enjoy. The chef wants to ensure that he shares his favorites with you that he has grown to love on his culinary journey.

### easy sweet and savory

Selected recipes will be noted **ESS** and will be 5 ingredients or less, minimal preparation and direction, and/or take less than 15 minutes to prepare for consumption. Most of the drinks will be an **ESS**, therefore, they will not be noted. We understand that good, healthy cuisine should not take long to prepare and you have busy lives. You deserve time to enjoy the good things in life, not take all day to prepare for them.

## food pairing

After the recipes, there may be food pairings to create complete meals or full dinners in courses. From aperitifs to desserts, check these to complete your dining experience. Chef Dana desires you have complete enjoyment of the culinary creations.

## libations pairing

Under food pairings, if any, there may be libations pairings for those that enjoy libations with their meals. With several courses, there may be several types of libations for your dining pleasure.

### chef's notes and culinary / pastry lessons

Some pages will include special educational lessons. They will vary from learning what a special herb or spice is to the different variations of custard. These are designed to enlighten and educate our readers on the wonderful world of food and hopefully connect some dots for some of our readers.

# contents

# desks .........................................................................................98

# beverages and cordials ................................................. 113

# food and libation parings

| Delectable Selections | Edible Pairing | Beverage Pairing |
|---|---|---|
| **Appetizers** | | |
| Chipotle Cinnamon Popcorn | | Botter Prosecco, Peach Nectar Bellini, or favorite moderate brown ale |
| Rosemary Fries | | Blue Moon beer |
| Fried Calamari with Pepper Aioli | | Mango Mojito or Blushing Virgin |
| Crabmeat Cheesecake | | Blackberry Mojito |
| Edamame | | Iced green tea with organic honey drizzle |
| Pretzel Bites with Sweet and Spicy Cream Cheese Dip | | Key Lime Pie or Miami Vice |
| Seared Scallop with Corn Cream Sauce | | Kim Crawford Sauvignon Blanc or Castle Rock Pinot Noir |
| **Breads and Muffins** | | |
| Apricot Rosemary Scone | | Domaine Chandon Brut Classic, favorite herbal tea or gourmet coffee |
| Mile High Butter Biscuit | | Favorite herbal tea or gourmet coffee |
| Sour Cream Blueberry Muffin | | Favorite herbal tea or gourmet coffee |
| Mom's Zucchini Bread | | Favorite herbal tea or gourmet coffee |
| Crumpets with Cinnamon Honey Butter and Preserves | Apricot Rosemary Scone | NV Roederer Estate Brut or Chandon Blush Champagne |
| **Breakfast for champions** | | |
| Crab Benedict | Mom's Zucchini Bread | Mimosa or a Weizen beer |
| Bacon and Cheddar Waffles | Sour Cream Blueberry Muffin | Orange juice, lemon herbal tea, gourmet coffee |
| Belgium Waffles with Fresh Raspberries and Raspberry Grand Marnier Syrup | Sour Cream Blueberry Muffin | Champagne cocktail with Chambord, Domaine Chandon Blanc de Noirs, or raspberry iced tea |
| Carrot Cake Waffle with Cinnamon Cream Cheese Spread | Mom's Zucchini Bread | Orange and Banana Mimosa |
| Banana Brulee French Toast | Sour Cream Blueberry Muffin | Orange or cranberry juice, or Banana |

| | | Mimosa |
|---|---|---|
| **Scrapple and Onion Omelet with Cheddar and American Cheese** | Mile High Butter Biscuit | Bloody Mary, a Weizen or best bitter |
| **Belgium Waffles with Maple Sausage and Caramel** | Sour Cream Blueberry Muffin or Apricot Rosemary Scone | Orange juice, lemon herbal tea, gourmet coffee, or Chandon Blush Champagne |
| **Egg In A Hole** | Sour Cream Blueberry Muffin or Mile High Butter Biscuit | Orange juice, lemon herbal tea, gourmet coffee, or Mumm Cuvee Champagne |
| **Chocolate Waffles** | Apricot Rosemary Scone | Peach Nectar Bellini or Roederer Estate Brut Rose |
| **Huevos and Chorizo con Chilaquilles (Eggs and Sausage with Tortillas)** | Mile High Butter Biscuit | Orange or cranberry juice, or Banana Mimosa |
| **Spicy Western Breakfast Tart** | Mile High Butter Biscuit | Orange or cranberry juice, or Mionetto Il Moscato |

## Dinner Delights

| | | |
|---|---|---|
| **Sweet and Spicy Wings** | Pretzel Bites with Sweet and Spicy Cream Cheese Dip, Brown Rice Pilaf or Chayote Squash, and Caramelized Banana Split | Strawberry Margarita, Blackberry Mojito, or Blushing Virgin |
| **Cola glazed Pork Tenderloin** | Tesha's Roasted Red Potatoes or Pecan Risotto with Golden Raisins, Carrot, Celery, and Apple Soup, and Poached Pear Salad with Chocolate Vinaigrette or Peach Cobbler | Penfolds Bin 389 2005 |
| **Kennett Square Mushroom Tart with Mache Salad and Truffle Vinaigrette** | Asparagus and Sun-dried Tomato Risotto or Butternut Squash Risotto, Vegetable Soup, and Lemon Curd | American Lemonade or Liberty School Cabernet Sauvignon |
| **Miso Glazed Sesame Salmon** | Snow Peas with Ginger or Strawberry, Watermelon, and Mozzarella with Balsamic Drizzle, Chicken Miso Soup, and Rosewater Crème Brulee | Patz and Hall Chardonnary |
| **Saffron and Lemon Risotto with Scallops** | Glazed Carrots or Carrots and Cabbage, Baby Spinach with Walnuts and Raisins, and Creamy Rice Pudding | Wente Riva Ranch Chardonnay 2008 |

## From the Garden to the Table

| | | |
|---|---|---|
| **Dana's House Salad with Mandarin Oranges, Red Onion, and White** | Cold Mango Soup | Botter or Bollinger Prosecco |

| | | |
|---|---|---|
| Chocolate Vinaigrette | | |
| Warm Spinach Salad with Mushrooms, Hard Boiled Egg, and Maple Bacon Dressing | Split Pea and Capp cola | Rued Russian River Chardonnay 2007 |
| Caesar Salad with Warm Parmesan Sabayon Dressing | Vegetable Soup | Kendall Jackson Vintners Reserve Sauvignon Blanc 2008 |
| Steak & Lobster Cobb Salad with Honey Mustard Dijon Vinaigrette | Cream of Pumpkin Soup | Cline Syrah or Mirassou Pinot Noir |
| Chop Chop Salad with Blueberry Truffle Vinaigrette | Chicken Miso Soup | Santa Margherita Pinot Grigio 2008 |
| Wedge Salad with Honeycomb and Applewood Bacon | Pear Brandy Shrimp Bisque | Cristom Vineyards Estate Pinot Gris 2006 |
| Watermelon, Mozzarella, Strawberry Salad | Watermelon Gazpacho | Duchessa Lia Barbera d"Asti 2007 |
| Poached Pear Salad with Chocolate Vinaigrette | Watermelon Gazpacho | Tangent Paragon Vineyard Abariño 2008 |
| Spinach Salad Sundried Cherries with Cherry Balsamic Vinaigrette | Carrot, Celery, and Apple Soup | Di Lenardo Pinot Grigio 2008 |

## Sandwiches

| | | |
|---|---|---|
| Ham and Swiss with Blueberry Chutney | Watermelon Gazpacho with Seasonal Berries and Pina Colada Dip | Hollinger Pinot Grigio 2008 |
| French Toasted Ham Sandwich with Blueberry Chutney | Carrot, Celery, and Apple Soup | Boston Cooler |
| Chicken Curry Salad Wrap | Vegetable Soup | Alta Vista Premium Torrontes 2008 |
| Grilled Tuna Sandwich with Sweet and Spicy Relish | Chicken Miso Soup | Bodega Sierra Cantabria Rioja Crianza 2005 |
| Flat Iron Steak Sandwich Onion Marmalade | Cream of Pumpkin Soup | Sterling Vineyards Cabernet Sauvignon |
| Smoked Turkey Sandwich with Apple Stuffing | Carrot, Celery, and Apple Soup | Glen Ellen Reserve Petite Sirah 2007 |
| Grilled Chicken Sandwich with Jicama Slaw | Cold Mango Soup and Sugar Cookies | Grand Tinel Chateauneuf du Pape 2005 |
| Grilled Turkey Reuben | Vegetable Soup and Almond Lace Cookies | Kaiken Ultra Malbec 2005 |

## Soups

| | | |
|---|---|---|
| Watermelon Gazpacho | (see Salads and Sandwiches selections) | Nassau Valley True Blue Blueberry (Sweet Red) |
| Cream of Pumpkin Soup with Cream Float | (see Salads and Sandwiches selections) | Jefferson Cabernet Franc 2007 |
| Chicken Miso Soup | (see Salads and Sandwiches selections) | Talbott Chardonnay Sleepy Hollow Monterey 2005 |
| Pear Brandy Shrimp Bisque | (see Salads and Sandwiches selections) | Trapiche Broquel Malbec 2007 or a Kölsch beer |
| Split Pea and Capp cola | (see Salads and Sandwiches selections) | Helfrich Gewurztraminer 2008 |
| Cold Mango Soup | (see Salads and Sandwiches selections) | Dry Creek Vineyard Sauvignon Blanc 2008 |
| Carrot, Celery, and Apple Soup | (see Salads and Sandwiches selections) | Whitehaven Sauvignon Blanc 2008 |
| Vegetable Soup | (see Salads and Sandwiches selections) | Ruffino Chianti 2008 or an English brown ale or porter beer |

## Dessert

| | | |
|---|---|---|
| Rosewater Crème Brule | (see Dinner Delights or Sandwich selections) | Ste. Michelle Reisling or Amalthea Cellars Late Harvest Villard |
| Lemon Curd | (see Dinner Delights or Sandwich selections) | Tokay or Be Friends Crémant Rosé |
| Creamy Rice Pudding | (see Dinner Delights or Sandwich selections) | Cake Bread Chardonnay |
| Chocolate Molten Cake with Vanilla Bean Ice Cream | (see Dinner Delights or Sandwich selections) | Layer Cake Shiraz 2008 or Trentadue Chocolate Amore |
| Sugar Cookies | (see Dinner Delights or Sandwich selections) | Nassau Valley Peach Ambrosia (Semi-Sweet White) |
| Texas Sheet Cake | (see Dinner Delights or Sandwich selections) | Nassau Valley House White (Sweet White) or Champagne |
| Pina Colada Dip | (see Dinner Delights or Sandwich selections) | Moet & Chandon Imperial |
| Caramelized Banana Split | (see Dinner Delights or Sandwich selections) | Nassau Valley Peach Ambrosia (Semi-Sweet White) |
| Almond Lace Cookies | (see Dinner Delights or Sandwich selections) | Favorite lemon or orange herbal tea |

| | | |
|---|---|---|
| **Peach Cobbler** | (see Dinner Delights or Sandwich selections) | Mionetto Il Moscato |

## The Sipping Sommelier

The Sipping Sommelier, L. Denise Jackson, is a much sought after speaker and trainer, published author, wine consultant, and founder of Wine Nouveau and The Sipping Sommelier blog. With an extremely discriminating nose and palate, she identifies aromas other sommeliers, including winemakers, overlook and she can pair wine with anything from a hot dog to Beluga caviar. She enjoys working with brides and their planners and dinner party hosts to create the best experience for their guests in expanding their appreciation of the wonderful world of wine. Helping people expand their wine familiarity is her specialty and her passion to keep the simple learning process is both evident and delightful.

L. Denise received her academic education from American University and the University of Maryland. As she continues her studies towards becoming a Master of Wine, she currently holds certifications in Wine and Spirits from the renowned Wine and Spirits Education Trust (WSET) and other certifying organizations and is a member of the Society of Wine Educators. Advanced studies and wine specialist certifications are in her near future. She holds regional wine dinners, consults clients and event planners nationally, and conducts the Sipping Sommelier Weekend Certification several times during the year. Residing in Washington, D.C., L. Denise enjoys reading, traveling, visiting family and friends, and always a delicious glass of wine with any meal.

*The Sipping Sommelier Blog is located at thesippingsommelier.blogspot.com can be reached at 202-302-3213 or at winenouveau@yahoo.com.*

## Liquid or Volume Measurements

| | | | | |
|---|---|---|---|---|
| jigger or measure | 1 1/2 or 1.5 fluid ounces | | 3 tablespoons | 45 ml |
| 1 cup | 8 fluid ounces | 1/2 pint | 16 tablespoons | 237 ml |
| 2 cups | 16 fluid ounces | 1 pint | 32 tablespoons | 474 ml |
| 4 cups | 32 fluid ounces | 1 quart | 64 tablespoons | .946 ml |
| 2 pints | 32 fluid ounces | 1 quart | 4 cups | .964 liters |
| 4 quarts | 128 fluid ounces | 1 gallon | 16 cups | 3.8 liters |
| 8 quarts | 256 fluid ounces or one peck | 2 gallons | 32 cups | 7.5 liters |
| 4 pecks | one bushel | | | |
| dash | less than 1/4 teaspoon | | | |

## Dry/Weight Measurements

| | | Ounces | Pounds | Metric |
|---|---|---|---|---|
| 1/16 teaspoon | a dash | | | |
| 1/8 teaspoon or less | a pinch or 6 drops | | . | .5 ml |
| 1/4 teaspoon | 15 drops | | | 1 ml |
| 1/2 teaspoon | 30 drops | | | 2 ml |
| 1 teaspoon | 1/3 tablespoon | 1/6 ounce | | 5 ml |
| 3 teaspoons | 1 tablespoon | 1/2 ounce | | 14 grams |
| 1 tablespoon | 3 teaspoons | 1/2 ounce | | 14 grams |
| 2 tablespoons | 1/8 cup | 1 ounce | | 28 grams |
| 4 tablespoons | 1/4 cup | 2 ounces | | 56.7 grams |
| 5 tablespoons plus 1 teaspoon | 1/3 cup | 2.6 ounces | | 75.6 grams |
| 8 tablespoons | 1/2 cup | 4 ounces | 1/4 pound | 113 grams |
| 10 tablespoons plus 2 teaspoons | 2/3 cup | 5.2 ounces | | 151 grams |
| 12 tablespoons | 3/4 cup | 6 ounces | .375 pound | 170 grams |
| 16 tablespoons | 1 cup | 8 ounces | .500 pound or 1/2 pound | 225 grams |
| 32 tablespoons | 2 cups | 16 ounces | 1 pound | 454 grams |
| 64 tablespoons | 4 cups or 1 quart | 32 ounces | 2 pounds | 907 grams |

# breakfast for champions

# crab benedict

Prep time: 10 minutes / Cook time: 15 minutes / Servings: 8

*Poached egg*

4 eggs

1 quart water

2 tbsp vinegar (white)

*Crab cake*

8 oz jumbo lump crabmeat

1 yellow pepper

1 tbsp finely chopped chives

1 cup panko bread crumbs

½ cup mayonnaise

salt and pepper to taste

2 tbsp oil

Creole mustard to taste

4 English muffins, to serve

1. Bring 1 quart water to a boil.
2. Reduce to a simmer and add vinegar.
3. In a bowl, combine all crab cake ingredients except the oil.
4. Heat the oil in a sauté pan.
5. Crack eggs into the simmering water and poach until done.
6. While eggs are poaching, form crab cakes and sauté until fully cooked.
7. Toast English muffins and place on a plate.
8. Top English muffin with crab cake.
9. Place poached eggs on crab cake.
10. Top with Creole hollandaise (recipe listed in sauces section).

# bacon and cheddar waffles

Prep time: 20 minutes / Cook time: 5 minutes / Servings: 10

1 egg

1 cup milk

1 cup sour cream

1 tbsp melted butter

4 oz apple wood bacon; cooked and crumbled

1 cup cheddar cheese, shredded

2 cups baking mix or self-rising flour

1. Beat egg.
2. Add milk, sour cream, and butter. Mix until combined.
3. Add baking mix and mix well.
4. Add apple wood bacon and cheddar cheese; stir.
5. Spoon batter into a hot waffle iron.
6. Cook until golden brown.

# belgian waffles with fresh raspberries and raspberry grand marnier syrup

Prep time: 10 minutes / Cook time: 20 minutes / Servings: 10

2 cups all-purpose flour

2 tsp baking powder

1 tbsp vegetable oil

2 tbsp confectioner sugar

2 cups milk

3 eggs, separated

2 tsp vanilla

salt to taste

butter to taste

1 pint fresh raspberries

2oz raspberry grand marnier syrup (*see sauce recipe*)

1. Combine the flour, baking powder, oil, sugar, milk and egg yolks.
2. In a separate bowl, beat egg whites and vanilla to a soft peak
3. Incorporate egg whites into the flour mixture, careful not to over mix.
4. Ladle 4 oz. batter onto hot waffle iron and cook (about 2 minutes).
5. Top with butter, fresh raspberries and raspberry Grand Marnier syrup.

# carrot cake waffle with cinnamon cream cheese spread

Prep time: 15 minutes / Cook time: 5 minutes / Servings: 4

*cinnamon cream cheese spread*

1 tsp cinnamon

8 oz cream cheese

8 oz butter

¼ cup confectioner sugar

*carrot cake waffle*

½ cup sugar

½ cup self-rising flour

¼ cup oats

½ tsp cinnamon

½ tsp baking soda

½ cup shredded carrot

¼ cup vegetable oil

1 egg, beaten

1 tbsp crushed pineapple

1 tbsp diced apple

1 tbsp raisins

*cinnamon cream cheese spread*

1. In a mixer blend cinnamon, cream cheese, butter and sugar until well combined.
2. Set aside.

*carrot cake waffle*

1. Combine all dry ingredients.
2. In a separate bowl mix the carrots, oil and eggs. Mix well.
3. Add wet mixture to dry ingredients until incorporated.
4. Fold in fruits.
5. Cook in waffle iron until golden brown.
6. Top waffle with cinnamon cream cheese spread.
7. Add your favorite syrup.

# banana Brule french toast

Prep time: 10 minutes / Cook time: 5 minutes / Servings: 4

3 eggs

4 cups milk

2 tsp cinnamon

¼ tsp nutmeg

1 tsp vanilla

2 tbsp sugar

1 oz oil

8 Texas toast slices

4 bananas

1 cup sugar

1. Preheat oven to 200°F

2. Mix eggs, milk, cinnamon, nutmeg, vanilla and sugar.

3. Heat oil in skillet or sauté plan to medium heat.

4. Dip one slice of bread at a time in the French toast batter and place in the heated sauté pan.

5. Cook until golden brown.

6. Flip French toast and cook until the second side is golden brown.

7. Place on an oven proof plate and put in the oven at 200°F. Add each piece to the plate until all of the French toast is done.

8. Slice bananas length wise and sprinkle with sugar.

9. Torch bananas with small torch.

10. Arrange 2 slices of French Toasts on a plate.

11. Top with 2 banana halves.

12. Pour on your favorite syrup and enjoy.

*I remember my grandmother had really thick syrup called King Syrup. I loved it so much! I buy a few bottles at a time when I find it to keep around. It's my favorite everyday syrup.*

# scrapple and onion omelet with cheddar or American cheese

Prep time: 10 minutes / Cook time: 8 minutes / Servings: 1

3 oz scrapple (thin sliced)

¼ oz onion (julienne)

3 eggs

1 oz sour cream (optional)

2 oz cheddar cheese (sliced)

2 oz American cheese (sliced)

1 oz vegetable oil

salt to taste

pepper to taste

truffle oil (optional)

1. Cook scrapple and set aside.

2. Sauté julienne onions in a little bit of butter and set aside.

3. Heat sauté pan with 1 oz oil over medium high heat.

4. Mix 3 eggs and sour cream well.

5. Pour egg mixture in the pan. Raise the edges of the omelet to allow the mixture to go under the cooked egg.

6. When egg is no longer runny, flip the egg. *This takes practice and a properly greased pan…it will come in time.*

7. Cook just until done. *Over cooking equals an omelet that doesn't fold well.*

8. Flip omelet back over and add sliced cheese and onions.

9. Place scrapple on one half of the omelet.

10. Fold the omelet and place on a plate.

11. Drizzle with a small amount of truffle oil.

# belgian waffle with maple sausage and salted caramel

Prep time: 10 minutes / Cook time: 5 minutes / Servings: 4

*waffle*

1 ¾ cups flour

2 tsp baking powder

1 tbsp sugar

½ tsp salt

3 egg yolks (beaten)

1 ¾ cups milk

½ cup vegetable oil

3 egg whites (beaten stiffly)

8 maple sausages

*salted caramel*

4 oz butter

8 oz brown sugar

1 cinnamon stick

8 oz heavy cream

1 tsp kosher salt

*belgian waffle*

1. Mix all dry ingredients.

2. In a separate bowl, combine yolks and milk.

3. Stir wet ingredients into dry ingredients.

4. Stir in oil and mix.

5. Gently fold in beaten egg whites, do not over mix.

6. Pour about ½ cup at a time into waffle iron.

7. In a sauté pan, cook the sausages until golden brown.

*salted caramel*

1. Heat butter and brown sugar in saucepan until melted. Add cinnamon stick.

2. Add heavy cream and allow to simmer 2 to 3 minutes.

3. Remove from heat and add salt.

*serve*

1. Place waffle on a plate.

2. Top waffle with a slice of sausage.

3. Drizzle the salted caramel on the sausage and waffle.

4. Enjoy.

# egg in a hole

Prep time: 3 minutes / Cook time: 5 minutes / Servings: 2

2 slices sandwich bread

2 tbsp butter

2 eggs

shredded pepper jack cheese

green onions, chopped

1. Using a 2 ½ inch biscuit cutter or a small glass, cut a round hole out of the center of the sandwich bread.

2. Melt butter in a large skillet over medium heat.

3. Add the bread slices and cook for about 30 seconds.

4. Crack the egg into the holes. *Do not worry if some of the white remains on top of the bread.*

   Add more butter if needed.

5. When the egg begins to set (2-3 minutes), flip the bread and egg.

6. Top the cooked side with pepper jack cheese and green onion.

7. Fry the other side until the eggs are done to your liking.

8. Serve on a warmed plate.

9. Fry the leftover rounds of bread and serve them as a side of toast.

# chocolate **waffles**

Prep time:10 minutes / Cook time: 10 minutes / Servings: 10

1 ½ cups flour

3 tsp baking powder

½ tsp salt

½ cup sugar

3 tbsp cocoa powder

1 cup milk

2 eggs

4 tbsp butter (melted)

*fondant icing*

1 tbsp butter (softened)

¾ cup confectioner sugar

½ tsp vanilla

2 tsp milk

*chocolate waffles*

1. Mix dry ingredients
2. Stir in milk, eggs, butter and mix until smooth
3. Mix together fondant icing. If too stiff add more milk.
4. Spray waffle iron with non-stick spray.
5. Pour mix into waffle iron.
6. Cook until golden brown.

*fondant icing*

1. Cream softened butter and sugar.
2. Add vanilla and milk; mix.

*serve*

Top waffle with fondant icing.

# huevos and chorizo con chilaquilles
## (eggs and sausage with tortillas)
Prep time: 10 minutes / Cook time: 10 minutes / Servings: 4

vegetable oil for frying

12 corn tortillas

3 green chilies, parched, peeled and finely chopped

3 large tomatoes, peeled, cut into thin wedges

1 medium-size onion, chopped

1 garlic clove, very finely chopped

⅛ tsp ground cumin

¼ tsp salt

freshly ground pepper

¼ lbs chorizo sliced

4 lightly fried or poached eggs (optional)

1 cup shredded Monterey jack cheese (optional)

1. Heat about ¼ inch oil in a large heavy skillet.
2. Cut the tortillas in half then into ¾ inch-wide strips.
3. Add strips to the hot oil and fry until almost crisp.
4. Drain on paper towels.
5. Combine the chilies, tomatoes, onion, garlic, cumin, salt, and pepper in a large saucepan.
6. Simmer about 5 minutes.
7. Add the tortilla strips and simmer 5 more minutes.
8. While vegetables are simmering, cook chorizo in skillet until done (hot).
9. Remove from pan.
10. Fry eggs over-easy or poach.
11. Spoon vegetable tortilla mix and chorizo onto plates.
12. Sprinkle with shredded cheese.
13. Top with egg for a hearty breakfast or brunch.

# spicy western **breakfast tart**

Prep time: 1 hour / Cook time: 40 min / Servings: 20

*tart dough*

4 cups flour

1 tbsp sugar

1 tsp baking powder

2 tsp salt

1 ¾ cup shortening

½ cup cold water

1 ea egg

1 tbsp vinegar

*filling*

8 slices pepper bacon

½ cup onion, diced

½ cup red pepper, diced

1 bunch green onion, chopped

⅓ cup cappicola

1 tbsp butter

3 cups heavy cream

8 ea eggs, beaten

¼ tsp salt

½ tsp black pepper

3 tbsp basil chopped

3 oz cream cheese, cubed

½ cup cheddar, shredded

½ cup pepper jack, shredded

*tart*

1. Mix together flour, sugar, baking powder and salt.

2. Cut in shortening until it is a coarse crumb.

3. Add water, egg and vinegar. Mix together until it comes together.

4. Divide in half and chill for an hour.

5. Preheat oven to 350 F

6. Form dough into a round and roll on a floured surface

7. Carefully fit the dough into two 10 inch tart pans.

8. Cook shell until golden brown.

9. Let cool.

10. Examine to make sure there are no holes.

*filling*

11. Cook bacon over medium heat until brown.

12. Drain and crumble.

13. Sauté onion, red pepper and green onion until translucent.

14. Divide bacon, cappicola and vegetable mixture into tart shells evenly.

15. Beat eggs and cream together. Add all seasonings and stir well.

16. Pour mixture over bacon and vegetable mixture in tart shells.

17. Sprinkle cream cheese cubes and shredded cheeses over the top.

18. Bake 40 minutes at 350 F

19. Allow to cool.

20. Cut and serve

# savory breakfast **bread pudding**

Prep time: 20 minutes / Cook time: 1 hour / Servings: 10

6 eggs

1 cup milk

½ cup heavy cream

1 tsp parsley

¼ tsp thyme

1  16oz loaf of bread, cubed

1 onion, diced

1 tsp garlic

1 cup sliced mushrooms

4 tbsp melted unsalted butter

6 maple turkey sausage, cooked and diced

1 cup shredded gouda cheese

½ cup fine dry bread crumbs

½ cup freshly grated parmesan

1. Preheat oven to 375°F (190°C).
2. Beat the eggs in a mixing bowl.
3. Whisk in the milk, cream, parsley and thyme until evenly blended.
4. Fold in the bread cubes and set aside until the bread soaks up the egg mixture, about 5 minutes.
5. Sauté the onions, garlic and mushrooms in 2 tbsp of butter in a small pan.
6. Add the sautéed ingredients to the bread mixture.
7. Fold in the turkey sausage and cheese.
8. Grease a 9x13 inch pan or casserole dish
9. Spoon the bread mixture into the dish.
10. Mix the remaining butter, parmesan cheese, and breadcrumbs
11. Sprinkle over the bread mixture.
12. Cover with aluminum foil.
13. Bake 40 minutes, or until the bread is no longer soggy.
14. Remove the foil and set the oven to Broil to give the pudding a beautiful golden color.

# buttermilk pancakes

Prep time: 10 minutes / Cook time: 15 minutes / Servings: 12

3 cups all-purpose flour

3 tbsp white sugar

3 tsp baking powder

1 ½  tsp baking soda

¾  tsp salt

3 cups buttermilk

½ cup milk

3 eggs

⅓ cup butter, melted

1 recipe lemon curd (*see desserts recipes*)

1 recipe boysenberry syrup

1. Heat a lightly oiled griddle over medium high heat.
2. In a large bowl, combine flour, sugar, baking powder, baking soda, and salt.
3. In a separate bowl, beat together buttermilk, milk, eggs and melted butter.
4. Pour the wet mixture into the dry mixture and mix quickly until just blended; careful not to over mix.
5. Pour or scoop ½ cup batter onto the griddle, for each pancake. Brown on both sides and serve hot.
6. As you cook each pancake, put a little bit of butter and lemon curd between each stacked pancake.
7. Top with a little boysenberry syrup.

# breads and muffins

# apricot rosemary scone

Prep time: 15 minutes / Cook time: 20 minutes / Yield: 2 dozen

4 cups flour

2 tbsp baking powder

1tsp salt

½ cup sugar

2 ½ cups heavy cream

½ cup dried apricot, chopped

1tsp rosemary, chopped

1. Preheat oven to 350°F.
2. Mix all dry ingredients in a mixer.
3. Slowly add heavy cream until combined.
4. Place dough on a floured surface.
5. Lightly knead in apricot and rosemary until ingredients are incorporated.
6. Roll out on a floured surface to a quarter inch thick.
7. Cut out scones.
8. Bake at 350°F for 20 minutes.

# mile high butter biscuit

Prep time: 15 minutes / Cook time: 25 minutes / Yield: 2 dozen

2 cups all-purpose flour

2 cups cake flour

2 tbsp sugar

2 tbsp baking powder

2 tsp salt

2 ½ cups heavy cream

⅔ cups melted butter (2 ½ sticks of butter)

1. Preheat oven to 350°F.
2. Mix all dry ingredients in a mixer with a paddle attachment.
3. Add heavy cream and mix until half incorporated
4. Slowly add butter; mix.
5. Scoop dough onto a baking sheet.
6. Bake approximately 25 minutes at 350°F.

# sour cream **blueberry muffins**

Prep time: 15 minutes / Cook time: 30 minutes / Yield: 2 dozen

2lbs 4 oz  granulated sugar

12 oz  unsalted butter

¼ oz salt

1 oz vanilla

1lb 6oz whole eggs

2lbs 8oz bread flour

1 ¼ oz baking soda

2 ½ lbs sour cream

2lbs frozen blueberries

1. Combine sugar, butter, salt and vanilla in a 20 quart mixing bowl with paddle attachment.

2. Mix 3 minutes on the 3$^{rd}$ speed until a smooth paste is formed, scraping bowl to incorporate all ingredients.

3. Mix 3 minutes on 1$^{st}$ speed; slowly add eggs until incorporated well, scrape down bowl.

4. Sift together flour and baking soda, add to mixer; mix for 2 minutes on the 1$^{st}$ speed or until the flour clears.

5. Add sour cream; mix 1 minute on the 2$^{nd}$ speed.

6. Fold in frozen berries by hand to prevent fruit damage and batter discoloration.

7. Scoop batter in a muffin pan (with liners).

8. Bake for 30 minutes at 350°F

**[1$^{st}$ speed=low; 2$^{nd}$ speed=med; 3$^{rd}$ speed=high]**

*One of my favorite muffins is the blueberry muffin.  This is a bakery quality recipe for blueberry muffins; you are going to love them. The muffins are very moist and delicious. (They become so moist from the sour cream). The batter is very versatile and can be used as a base and substituted with other flavors. (Lemon Poppy Seed, Lavender, Cranberry Orange, just to name a few).  This is a very simple recipe and these muffins should come out beautiful, even if you are new to baking.*

# mom's zucchini bread

Prep time: 20 minutes / Cook time: 1 hour / Servings: 24

3 cups all-purpose flour

1 tsp salt

1 tsp baking powder

1 tsp baking soda

¼ tsp nutmeg

3 tsp ground cinnamon

3 eggs

1 cup vegetable oil

3 tsp vanilla extract

2 ¼ cups white sugar

1 ½ cups grated zucchini

½ cup carrot shredded

½ cup raisins

1 cup chopped walnuts

1. Preheat oven to 325°F (165°C).

2. Grease and flour two 8x4 inch pans.

3. In a bowl, sift together flour, salt, baking powder, baking soda, nutmeg and cinnamon.

4. Beat eggs, oil, vanilla, and sugar together in a large bowl.

5. Add sifted ingredients to the creamed mixture, and beat well.

6. Stir in zucchini, carrot, raisins and walnuts until well combined.

7. Pour batter into prepared pans.

8. Bake for 40-60 minutes or until tester inserted in the center comes out clean.

9. Cool in pan on rack for 20 minutes.

10. Remove the bread from the pan, and cool completely.

# crumpets with cinnamon honey butter and preserves

Prep time: 20 minutes / Cook time: 5 minutes / Servings: 4

3 tbsp warm water

1 pkg. yeast

1 tsp sugar

½ cup milk

4 tbsp butter, divided

½ tsp salt

1 ½ cup flour

1 egg

1. Combine water, yeast and sugar. Let stand about 5 minutes.

2. Heat milk, 1 tbsp butter and salt in a saucepan over low heat until warm. Add to yeast mixture.

3. Add 1 cup flour to yeast mixture and beat on medium speed until smooth.

4. Add egg and mix until incorporated.

5. Add remaining flour and beat until smooth.

6. Cover batter and let rise in a warm place until size is doubled.

7. Stir batter and let rest approximately 5 minutes.

8. Melt remaining butter in a saucepan over low heat; skim off foam and milky solids.

9. Brush bottom of a skillet with melted butter.

10. Brush insides of 3-inch round cookie cutters with butter and place rings in the prepared skillet.

11. Heat skillet over medium heat.

12. Spoon about 2 tbsp of batter into each ring.

13. Cook until batter begins to bubble on top and is lightly browned on the bottom.

14. *Careful, hot:* Remove rings.

15. Turn crumpets over and cook until lightly browned on bottom and done in the centers.

*serve*

1. Serve warm

2. Add Cinnamon Honey Butter and Preserves.

# chocolate cherry bread

Prep time: 20 minutes / Cook time: 25 minutes / Servings: 16

1 cup warm water

1 tbsp sugar

1 packet dry instant yeast

2 ⅓ cup all-purpose flour

⅓ cup sugar

⅓ cup cocoa powder

1 tsp salt

½ cup chocolate chips

1 ½ cups sundried cherries, soaked

1. Mix warm water, 1 tbsp sugar, and instant yeast. Set aside for 5 minutes or until the yeast gets foamy (activated).

2. In a large bowl, sift together flour, sugar, cocoa powder, and salt.

3. Add the flour mixture, then the yeast mixture to a food processor with the dough attachment or blade.

4. Add 1 tbsp melted butter.

5. Process into smooth and elastic dough.

6. Knead briefly on a well-floured surface and pat down to a square.

7. Sprinkle with 1/2 cup chocolate chips (*I use bittersweet*) and the sundried cherries.

8. Knead well to evenly distribute chocolate and cherries within the dough.

9. Place the dough in a large bowl; allow to rise for 1 to 1 ½ hours.

10. After the dough has risen, punch it down. Cover and set it in the fridge overnight.

11. Shape the dough into a log and make 16 equal pieces. *The easiest way is to divide the log into fourths, then divide each fourth into quarters.*

12. Shape each piece into a ball and set on a non-stick baking sheet.

13. Allow the dough to rise.

14. Pre-heat the oven to 375 F.

15. Bake the rolls for 20-25 minutes.

*For best results, serve warm.*

# appetizers

# chipotle and cinnamon sugar popcorn

Prep time: 5 minutes / Cook time: 2 minutes / Yield: 1 lb

1 tbsp cinnamon

½ cup sugar

½ tbsp chipotle

1 lb your favorite plain popcorn

¼ cup melted Butter

1. Combine cinnamon, sugar, and chipotle in a bowl.
2. In a large bowl combine popcorn and butter.
3. Add cinnamon sugar spice and toss well.

*This is a MAJOR hit for TV Time!!! Everyone loves it and it's **so** simple to make.*

# rosemary fries

Prep time: 20 minutes / Cook time: 45 minutes / Servings: 4

*fries*

5 russet potatoes cut into wedges

3 tbsp olive oil

pepper to taste

*rosemary salt*

1 cup rosemary

5 tbsp salt

1 tbsp garlic powder

1 lb light brown sugar (dry)

*fries*

1. Preheat oven to 350°F
2. Combine potato, oil, and pepper on a sheet pan.
3. Bake for 40 to 45 minutes.

*rosemary salt*

4. Combine rosemary and salt in a small food processor and blend well. *Grind it well; almost to a powder.*
5. Transfer to an air tight container and add garlic powder and brown sugar.
6. Set aside
7. Remove potatoes when done and toss immediately with the rosemary salt to taste.

*Note: To dry brown sugar spread flat on a sheet pan and dry for 3 days at room temp. This will make a fine salt.*

# fried calamari with pepper aioli

Prep time:35 minutes / Cook time: 1 minute / Servings: 4

¼ cup cornmeal or cornstarch

1 cup breadcrumb

salt to taste

1tbsp old bay seasoning

2 eggs, slightly beaten

2 cloves garlic, mashed

1lb cleaned calamari, cut into rings

oil (for frying)

1 recipe pepper aioli(*see sauces, dressings and marmalades*)

1 recipe sambal sauce(*see sauces, dressings and marmalades*)

1. Place cornmeal in a shallow dish.

2. In a separate shallow dish, mix together breadcrumbs, salt and old bay seasoning.

3. In a bowl, combine egg and garlic.

4. Coat calamari rings in corn meal; shake off excess cornmeal.

5. Dredge calamari in the egg mixture, and then dip them in the breadcrumb mixture. Coat well, shake off excess coating.

6. Meanwhile, heat the oil to just below the smoking point.

7. Carefully add the calamari to the oil.

8. Fry the rings about 1 minute, or until golden brown. (*The secret to crispy calamari is hot, hot oil*)

9. Remove and drain on paper towels.

10. Serve immediately with lemon wedges, chili pepper aioli and sambal sauce.

*Note: A deep fryer is best; otherwise make sure the oil is deep enough to cover the calamari*

# crabmeat cheesecake with pecan crust

Prep time: 1 hour / Cook time: 50 minutes / Servings: 9

*pecan crust*

¾ cup pecans

1 cup all-purpose flour

½ tsp salt

5 tbsp unsalted butter, cold

3 tbsp ice water

*filling*

½ small onion, finely diced

4 oz fresh lump crabmeat, picked over for shells

8 oz cream cheese, room temperature

3 oz Creole cream cheese (or 3 tbsp each plain yogurt and sour cream

2 eggs

salt and white pepper to taste

crystal hot sauce to taste (*or your favorite hot sauce*)

*garnish*

3 tbsp unsalted butter, softened

2 tbsp chopped shallots

4 oz sliced mixed wild and exotic mushrooms

1 tbsp lemon juice

3 oz Worcestershire sauce

1 oz hot sauce

3 oz heaving whipping cream

24 crab claw fingers

salt and freshly ground black pepper to taste

*pecan crust*

1. Preheat oven to 350° F

2. Finley grind pecans, flour and salt in a food processor.

3. Transfer to a bowl and add the butter.

4. Work the butter into the flour until you have crumbs about the size of a pea.

5. Add ice water, lifting up the dough with your fingers to incorporate evenly. (*The dough will remain fairly crumbly*).

6. Starting with the sides, and then the bottom, press the dough into a 9-inch tart pan.

7. Bake the crust for 20 minutes.

8. Allow the crust to cool before filling.

*filling*

1. Cook the onion in a bit of butter over medium heat until translucent. Add the crabmeat and cook until heated through.

2. Remove from heat and set aside.

3. In a mixer fitted with the paddle attachment (or by hand using a wooden spoon), blend the cream cheese until smooth. Add the Creole cream cheese, then the eggs one at a time.

4. Fold in the crabmeat mixture. Season to taste with salt, white pepper and hot sauce.

5. Pour the mix into the prepared cooled crust.

6. Bake at 300° F for 30 minutes until set and firm to the touch.

*garnish topping*

1. Sautee shallots in butter until translucent. Add the mushrooms and sweat until just cooked through.

2. Add the lemon juice, Worcestershire sauce and hot sauce, and reduce by ¾.

3. Add the heavy cream and reduce by half. Whisk in the butter.

4. In a separate sauté pan, add crab claw fingers. Salt and pepper to taste, then pour the reduction over and keep warm.

5. Each slice of cheesecake gets three crab claws and 2 tablespoon of sauce.

# Edamame

Prep time: 5 minutes / Cook time: 4 min / Servings: 4

½ lb fresh edamame

1 tsp coarse sea salt

¼ tsp ground black pepper

*alternate spicy seasoning*

1 tsp salt

¼ tsp pepper

¼ tsp old bay seasoning

1. Steam edamame for 3-4 minutes until done.

2. Remove and toss with salt and pepper

*Note: frozen can be used if fresh is unavailable.*

# seared scallop with corn cream sauce

Prep time: 15 minutes / Cook time: 30 minutes / Servings: 4

1 cup vegetable stock

2 tbsp onion

3 tbsp red pepper

1 tomato, chopped

4 cups corn

1 clove garlic

1 bay leaf

2 sprigs cilantro

¼ cup cream

¼ cup evaporated milk

2 tsp cornstarch

1 tbsp water

1 tbsp butter; softened

8 large scallops

4 tbsp maple syrup

4 ea cooked bacon, diced

1. Sauté vegetables and seasonings until tender in vegetable stock.

2. Remove from heat to cool.

3. Remove bay leaf

4. Puree in a blender or food processor.

5. Strain into a saucepan.

6. Add heavy cream and evaporated milk.

7. Mix together cornstarch and water.

8. Add to the saucepan. Stirring constantly.

9. When thickened, add butter and stir. Set aside.

10. Sear large scallops until done. Brush with maple syrup.

*serve*

1. Place a little sauce in the center of each plate.

2. Place scallops on the sauce.

3. Top with bacon and a little drizzle of maple syrup.

*"There is no love sincerer than the love of food."*
George Bernard Shaw, Irish playwright (1856-1950)

# pretzel bites with sweet and spicy cream cheese dip

Prep time: 2 hours / Cook time: 10 min / Servings: 12

4 tsp active dry yeast

1 tsp white sugar

1 ¼ cups warm water

4 cups all-purpose flour

½ cup white sugar

1 ½ tsp salt

1 tbsp vegetable oil

½ cup baking soda

4 cups hot water

¼ cup kosher salt, for topping

*cream cheese dip*

1 lb cream cheese, softened

3 tbsp Asian sweet chili sauce

*pretzels*

1. In a small bowl, dissolve yeast and 1 tsp sugar in warm water. Let stand until creamy, about 10 minutes.

2. In a large bowl, mix together flour, ½ cup sugar, and salt.

3. Make a well in the center; add the oil and yeast mixture. Mix and form into a ball of dough. *If the mixture is dry, add one or two tablespoon of water.*

4. Knead the dough until smooth, about 7-8 minutes.

5. Place the dough in a lightly oiled large bowl, turning to coat with oil. Cover with plastic wrap and let rise in a warm place until doubled in size, about 1 hour.

6. Preheat oven to 450°F.

7. In a large bowl, dissolve baking soda in hot water.

8. When dough has risen, turn out onto a lightly floured surface and divide into 24 to 36 equal pieces.

9. Roll each piece into a pretzel shape.

10. Dip each pretzel into the baking soda solution and place on a greased baking sheet.

11. Sprinkle with kosher salt.

12. Bake in preheated oven for 8 minutes, until browned.

*dip*

13. Mix ingredients together.

14. Set aside in refrigerator until ready to use.

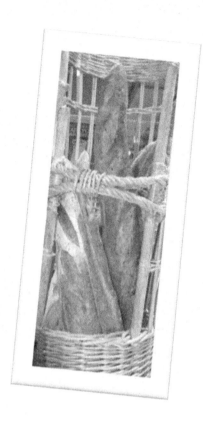

# soups

# watermelon gazpacho

Prep time: 5 minutes / Cook time: 0 minutes / Servings: 6

2 cups ¼ inch diced watermelon

1 cup strawberries

2 cups fresh squeezed orange juice

2 tbsp extra-virgin olive oil

1 seedless cucumber, cut ¼ inch dice

1 small yellow bell pepper, seeded & cut ¼ inch dice

1 small onion, cut into ¼ inch dice

1 cup black berries

2 medium garlic cloves, minced

1 small jalapeno pepper, seeded & minced (optional)

3 tbsp fresh lime juice

2 tbsp chopped fresh parsley, basil or cilantro

salt and freshly ground black pepper to taste

1. Blend together ½ cup watermelon, ½ cup strawberries, orange juice and oil until pureed.

2. Transfer to a medium bowl.

3. Add remaining ingredients and mix.

4. Season with salt and pepper to taste.

5. Refrigerate until ready to serve.

# cream of pumpkin soup with cream float

Prep time: 20 minutes / Cook time: 40 minutes / Servings: 4

6 cups chicken stock

1 ½ tsp salt

4 cups pumpkin puree

1 cup chopped onion

½ tsp chopped fresh thyme

1 garlic clove, minced

5 whole black peppercorns

1 tsp chopped fresh parsley

1 tsp cinnamon

1 tbsp vanilla

2 tbsp brown sugar

1 ½ cup heavy whipping cream

1. Heat stock, salt, pumpkin, onion, thyme, garlic, and peppercorns. Bring to a boil, reduce heat to low, and simmer for 30 minutes uncovered.

2. Allow to cool.

3. Puree the soup in small batches (*1 cup at a time using a food processor or blender*).

4. Return to pan, and return to a boil.

5. Add cinnamon, vanilla and brown sugar and reduce heat to low.

6. Simmer for 30 minutes, uncovered.

7. Stir in 1/2C heavy cream.

8. Whip remaining cup of heavy whipping cream to a soft peak. Pour into a sauce bottle.

9. Pour soup into bowls and garnish with sauce in a spiral design and parsley.

*What I love about Pumpkin Soup is when summer has gone, fall has begun and the temperature begins to drop, nothing warms you up like pumpkin soup.*

# chicken miso soup

Prep time: 10 minutes / Cook time: 15 minutes / Servings: 2

2 tsp dashi granules

4 cups water

3 tbsp miso paste

1 (8oz) package silken tofu, diced

2 green onions, sliced diagonally into ½ inch pieces

8oz chicken breast grilled and diced

1. In a medium saucepan over medium heat, bring dashi granules and water to a boil.
2. Reduce heat to medium, whisk in miso paste
3. Stir in tofu.
4. Separate the layers of the green onions, and add to the soup
5. Simmer gently for 2 to 3 minutes before serving.

---

*Colors of Miso*

**How old is your miso?**

How long the miso has been fermented is what gives it the particular color. Miso paste can be fermented for as little as one month or as much as three years.

**White** - very light flavor. Best for light cooking and summer soups.

**Yellow** - a bit saltier and stronger than White. A good intensity for moderate soups and sauces.

**Red** - saltier and stronger in flavor than Yellow. Favored for winter soups.

**Dark Brown** or **Black** - very strong flavor and smell. Best for rich cooking, such as with meat or stews.

# pear brandy **shrimp bisque**

Prep time: 15 minutes / Cook time: 20 minutes / Servings: 4

2lbs shell-on shrimp

4 tbsp unsalted butter (½ stick)

2 medium yellow onions, large dice

2 medium carrots, large dice

2 medium stalks celery, large dice

2 tbsp tomato paste

5 fresh thyme sprigs

2 medium bay leaves

5 cups water

3 tbsp all-purpose flour

½ pear brandy

¾ cup heavy cream

¼ tsp cayenne pepper

1. Peel Shrimp, reserving shells.

2. Coarsely chop shrimp into bite-size pieces, place in a medium container, cover, and refrigerate until ready to use.

3. Place 1 Tbsp of butter in a large saucepan over medium heat. When the foaming subsides, add onion, carrots, celery, and reserved shrimp shells. Season with salt and freshly ground black pepper.

4. Cook stirring occasionally, until onions are tender and shells are pink, but not browned (*approximately 5 minutes*).

5. Increase heat to medium-high and add tomato paste, thyme and bay leaves; stir until vegetables are coated in tomato paste.

6. Add water, stir to combine, and bring to a boil.

7. Reduce heat to a low simmer until broth has shrimp flavor (*approximately 30 minutes*).

8. Strain through a fine mesh strainer into a heatproof container; set aside and discard solids.

9. Wipe out any solids in the saucepan and return to the stove over low heat.

10. Add remaining butter and let melt. When butter foams, whisk in flour and cook, whisking frequently, until smooth and golden brown (*approximately 4 minutes*).

11. Slowly whisk in Cognac, then reserved hot stock. Whisk until smooth, and bringing to a boil.

12. Add cream, cayenne, and reserved shrimp and stir to combine. Simmer until flavors have melded and shrimp is cooked through but not tough (*about 8 to 10 minutes*).

13. Season with salt and freshly ground black pepper, if desired.

# split pea and cappicola

Prep time: 5 minutes / Cook time: 2 hours / Servings: 6

1 cup chopped onion

1 tsp vegetable oil

1lb dried split peas

1lb cappicola, diced

salt and pepper to taste

1. In medium pot, sauté onions in oil or bacon grease.

2. Remove from heat and add split peas and cappicola.

3. Add enough water to cover ingredients. Season with salt and pepper.

4. Cover, and cook until peas have liquefied (approximately *2hours*) *While cooking, check to see if the water has evaporated; add more water as the soup continues to cook.*

5. Once the soup is a green liquid, remove from heat, and let stand to thicken.

6. Once thickened, if necessary, reheat to serve.


# cold mango soup

Prep time: 15 minutes / Cook time: 0 minutes / Servings: 6

6 cups mango, ripe

2 cups apricot nectar

3 tbsp honey

2 cups dry champagne

1 cup whipping cream

fresh mint leaves (garnish)

1. Finely chop 1 ½ cups of mango. Set aside.

2. Blend remaining coarsely chopped mango with honey. *This should only take a few seconds.* Pour into a large bowl.

3. Stir in champagne and reserved mango.

4. Cover and refrigerate until ready to serve.

5. Pour into iced bowls.

6. Whip cream to soft peaks and use as a garnish with fresh mint leaves.

# carrot, celery and apple soup

Prep time: 20 minutes / Cook time: 40 minutes / Servings: 4

2lbs carrot

1 onion, chopped

3 celery, stalks

2 cups apple juice

2 cups vegetable stock

3 apples, medium

2 tbsp tomato paste

¼ cup brown sugar

1 bay leaf

3 tbsp sugar

½ tbsp cinnamon

½ tsp nutmeg

1. Place the carrots, onions, and celery in a large pot with the apple juice and vegetable stock.

2. Bring to a boil, and then reduce the heat to a simmer. Simmer for 10 minutes.

3. While the pot is simmering, peel and core the apples. Dice the apples and add them to the pot along with the tomato paste, brown sugar, bay leaf, and sugar. Return the pot to a boil over medium heat.

4. Reduce the heat to a simmer and cover for 10 minutes. Remove and discard the bay leaf.

5. Allow soup to cool. Place the mixture in a food processor and blend until smooth.

6. Return the soup to a clean pot and heat gently.

7. Season with salt and pepper.

8. Ladle the soup into warm bowls.

# vegetable soup

Prep time: 15 minutes / Cook time: 30 minutes / Servings: 6

1 tbsp olive oil

1 medium onion, chopped

2 carrots, sliced

2 stalks celery, sliced

6 ea diced plum tomatoes

1 tsp basil

1 tsp oregano

2 cubes beef bouillon

6 cups water

1 cup fresh squeezed orange juice

2 cups sliced cabbage

1 tsp garlic salt

salt and ground black pepper to taste

freshly grated parmesan cheese (optional)

1. Heat oil in a large stock pot over medium-high heat. Sauté onion, carrot, and celery until onion is translucent and vegetables are tender (*5-7 minutes*).

2. Stir in tomatoes, basil and oregano. Cook 5 more minutes, stirring frequently.

3. Dissolve bouillon cubes in water, and stir into vegetables.

4. Add orange juice. Adjust heat to a medium simmer, and cook approximately 10 minutes.

5. Add cabbage, sprinkle with garlic salt, and cook until tender ( *5 minutes*).

6. Adjust seasoning with salt and pepper, and serve.

*Note: juice must be squeezed from a fresh orange.*

# from the garden to the table

# dana's house salad with white chocolate orange vinaigrette

Prep time: 15 minutes / Cook time: 5 minutes / Servings: 4

1 recipe white chocolate orange dressing*(see sauces, dressings and marmalades)*

1 cup mandarin oranges

1/3 cup sliced onions

1/4 cup toasted almonds

1 ea kiwis, peeled and sliced

1 ea champagne mango peeled and diced

10 cups mescaline spring mix

7. Mix ingredients in a bowl. Tossing them lightly

8. Drizzle white chocolate dressing lightly over salad and serve

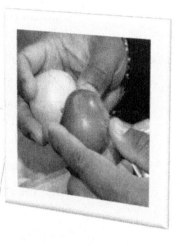

# warm spinach salad with miso maple bacon dressing

Prep time: 20 minutes / Cook time: 10 minutes / Servings: 4

8oz. young spinach

2 ea large eggs, hard boiled and sliced

4 ea large white mushrooms, sliced thin

1 ea granny smith apple, diced small

3 oz. red onion, thinly sliced

*dressing*

1 tbsp white miso

2 tbsp rice wine vinegar

1 tbsp mirin

1 tsp maple syrup (pure)

pinch of cayenne

1 slice thick cut bacon

*salad*

1. Wash and dry spinach greens. Pick stems if necessary.

2. Mix eggs, vegetables, apple and spinach. Set aside.

*dressing*

1. In a small bowl mix miso, vinegar, maple syrup and cayenne. Set aside.

2. Cut bacon into a small dice. Cook bacon slowly in a frying pan until crispy. Remove pieces and reserve oil in pan.

3. Add miso mixture to the pan with bacon grease and cook until slightly thickened.

*serve*

Drizzle warm dressing over salad. Toss to coat. Top with bacon.

# caesar salad with warm parmesan sabayon dressing

Prep time: 45 minutes / Cook time: 15 minutes / Servings: 8

*puff pastry twists*

1 ea egg

1 tbsp water

¼ cup grated parmesan cheese

1 tbsp chopped fresh parsley

½ tsp dried oregano leaves, crushed

½ tsp red pepper flakes

½ 17.3-ounce package of puff pastry sheets (1 sheet), thawed

*parmesan sabayon*

4 large egg yolks

¼ cup dry white vermouth

¼ cup fresh lemon juice

½ tsp Dijon mustard

¾ tsp kosher salt

small pinch cayenne pepper

1 tbsp grated asiago cheese

¼ cup chopped cilantro

2 ea medium heads of romaine lettuce, quartered lengthwise

1. Preheat oven to 400°F.

2. Beat the egg and water in a small bowl.

3. In a separate small bowl, stir the cheese, parsley, oregano, and red pepper.

4. Unfold the pastry sheet onto a lightly floured surface. *This is important as you do not want the puff pastry to stick to the surface.* Roll the pastry sheet into a 14x10-inch rectangle.

5. Cut the puff pastry in half lengthwise. Brush each half with the egg mixture.

6. Top one half with the cheese mixture. Invert the egg washed puff pastry half over the cheese coated half, egg-side down. Roll gently with a rolling pin to seal.

7. Cut the puff pastry into 28 (1/2 inch) strips.

8. Twist the strips and place on a baking sheet, pressing down the ends.

9. Brush the pastries with the egg mixture.

10. Bake for 10 minutes or until the puff pastry twists are a golden brown. Remove the pastries from the baking sheets and let cool.

11. Bing 2 inches of water to a boil in a saucepan. Choose a medium-sized stainless steel mixing bowl that will fit on top of the saucepan; *the bottom should not touch the water*.

12. Whisk the egg yolks with the vermouth, lemon juice, mustard, salt, and cayenne in the mixing bowl.

13. Place the bowl over the boiling water and whisk vigorously until the sabayon becomes very thick and fluffy (*about 2 to 3 minutes*).

14. Add the parmesan and cilantro.

15. Place romaine quarter and parmesan twist on the plate.

16. Top with parmesan sabayon.

17. Serve immediately.

# steak & lobster cobb salad with honey mustard dijon vinaigrette

Prep time: 15 minutes / Cook time: 10 minutes / Servings: 3

*honey mustard vinaigrette*

2 tbsp champagne vinegar

3 tbsp honey

2 tbsp Dijon mustard

1 garlic clove, minced

¼ tsp salt

¼ tsp ground black pepper

½ cup grape seed oil

*salad*

3 eggs; hard boiled

1 tbsp white vinegar

4 cups chopped romaine lettuce

2 cups iceberg lettuce, chopped

1 ½ cup arugula

1 tomato, diced

½ cup chopped tarragon

½ cup chopped scallions

¼ cup grated cheddar

¼ cup grated asiago

3 tbsp olive oil, extra virgin

1 ½ lbs cooked lobster

1 ½ lbs flank steak

1 ea avocado, peeled, pitted and diced

6 ea slices, maple pepper bacon, cooked and diced

*dressing*

1. In a food processor or blender, mix the vinegar, honey, mustard, garlic, salt and pepper

2. While mixing, slowly add grape seed oil until incorporated.

*salad*

1. For the eggs, start with enough cold water to cover the eggs. Add vinegar.

2. Bring water to a boil over medium heat.

3. Reduce heat to low and cook for 3 minutes.

4. Removes eggs from water and place in an ice bath.

5. In a mixing bowl, toss together salad greens, herbs, scallions and cheese. Set aside in refrigerator.

6. Heat olive oil to medium heat. Add lobster meat and cook until done. Remove to cutting board and cut into slices.

7. Cook flank steak until medium rare and allow to rest 5-10 minutes. Cut into slices.

8. Remove the greens from the refrigerator.

9. Add salt and pepper.

10. Top the salad with lobster, steak, avocado, tomato, eggs and bacon.

11. Serve immediately.

# chop chop salad with blueberry truffle vinaigrette

Prep time: 10 minutes / Cook time: 0 minutes / Servings: 6

*salad*

1 romaine lettuce heart

4 to 6 slices thick-cut bacon, cooked until crisp, cooled and chopped

½ pint grape tomatoes, halved

2 carrots, peeled and thinly sliced

1 yellow bell pepper, chopped

1 English cucumber, halved lengthwise and thinly sliced

½ cup chopped walnuts

coarse salt and freshly ground pepper to taste

*dressing*

½ cup blueberries, fresh or frozen (but fresh is best)

1 tbsp apple juice

2 tbsp red or white wine vinegar

2 tbsp soy yogurt (or use water or additional apple juice)

1 tsp shallots, coarsely chopped

⅛ tsp salt

1 pinch stevia (or other sweetener, to taste)

freshly ground black pepper to taste

1. Chop the lettuce heart into 1-2 inch pieces.

2. Combine lettuce with the bacon, vegetables, and nuts in a large bowl and toss to mix well.

3. Keep the salad chilled until serving time.

4. Puree all dressing ingredients in a blender until relatively smooth.

5. Drizzle over salad

6. Toss the salad to ensure the dressing covers the vegetables; season with salt and pepper.

7. Serve.

# watermelon, mozzarella, strawberry salad

Prep time: 15 minutes / Cook time: 30 minutes / Servings: 8

balsamic reduction

2 cups balsamic vinegar

½ cup honey


salad

4 cups watermelon

1 lb mozzarella sliced

4 cups strawberries sliced

1 tbsp basil chiffonade

salt and pepper to taste

1. Combine vinegar and honey in a saucepan and boil until it has reduced to ½ cup and reaches a syrup-like consistency. Let cool.

2. Arrange ingredients as desired. *I like sliced.*

3. Drizzle with balsamic syrup.

4. Top with basil chiffonade.

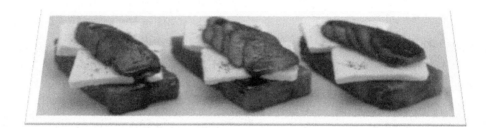

# wedge salad with honeycomb and apple wood bacon

Prep time: 10 minutes / Cook time: 5 minutes / Servings: 4

*bacon blue cheese dressing*

1 cup mayo

4 oz blue cheese

3 tbsp milk

2 tbsp lemon juice

1 tbsp finely chopped onion

¼ cup rendered bacon fat

3 tsp sugar

¼ tsp Worcestershire sauce

¼ tsp dry mustard

¼ tsp salt


*salad*

1 ea head iceberg, cut into quarters

1 ea tomato, finely diced

½ cup crumbled blue cheese

1 cup cooked applewood bacon, diced (slow cook and render the fat. save for the dressings)

¼ cup honeycomb, broken up

1. Render bacon and reserve the fat for dressing. Put bacon pieces aside.

2. For dressing mix all ingredients in a food processor except the rendered fat. Once mixed, slowly drizzle in the rendered fat.

3. Place salad wedge on a plate on its side.

4. Drizzle dressings over the salad wedge.

5. Top with tomato, crumbled blue cheese, bacon and honeycomb.

# poached pear salad with chocolate vinaigrette

Prep time: 35 minutes / Cook time: 10 minutes / Servings: 8

1 cup red wine

⅓ cup sugar

¼ cup water

½ tsp whole cloves

1 ea star anise

1 inch cinnamon stick

1 vanilla bean, halved lengthwise (optional)

4 firm, ripe pears, peeled

10 cups mescaline spring mix

⅔ cup dried tart cherries or dried cranberries

½ cup broken walnuts, toasted

1 recipe white chocolate vinaigrette*(see sauces, dressings and marmalades)*

1. In a medium pot, combine red wine, sugar, water, cloves, anise, cinnamon stick, and vanilla bean. Bring to a boil over medium heat, stirring to dissolve sugar; reduce heat.

2. Carefully add peeled pears to the pot, cover and simmer for 8 to 10 minutes or until pears are tender (*test for doneness by inserting a wooden toothpick into the thickest part of a pear. The pears should still be slightly firm, but the wooden pick should penetrate easily*).

3. Remove from heat immediately. Drain pears, reserve the liquid and spices. Transfer the pears to a bowl. Cover and chill in the refrigerator for 2 hours.

4. Return the reserved liquid to the pot and reduce by half until it reaches a syrup-like consistency. Cool syrup in the refrigerator. Prepare the Chocolate Vinaigrette.

5. To serve salad, in a large bowl, combine mescaline, half of the cherries or cranberries, and half of the toasted walnuts. Pour half of the dressing over salad mixture; toss lightly to coat. Set aside.

6. Place a sliced pear half on each salad plate. Place some of the dressed mescaline in the center of each plate.

7. On each serving, drizzle a little more vinaigrette and sprinkle with remaining cherries or cranberries and walnuts.

# spinach salad with cherry balsamic vinaigrette

Prep time: 15 minutes / Cook time: 12 minutes / Servings: 8

1 cup frozen sweet cherries, thawed and drained

½ cup balsamic vinegar

1 tbsp chopped shallots

1 tbsp honey

1 tbsp apple cider

salt and pepper, to taste

3 tbsp grape seed oil

1 cup granulated sugar

1 egg white

1 tbsp salt

1 tsp cayenne pepper

1 cup pecans

1 cup pine nuts

1 lb baby spinach, cleaned

4 oz blue cheese, crumbled

¼ cup sundried cherries

1. Combine cherries, vinegar, shallots, honey, cider, salt and pepper in a blender. Puree dressing until smooth. Slowly drizzle in the oil.

2. In a medium bowl, combine sugar and egg white. Stir in 1 tbsp salt and cayenne pepper.

3. Add pecans and pine nuts, coating them evenly.

4. Spread pecans evenly on a baking sheet with parchment paper.

5. Cook 350 F for 12 minutes or until done. Place on a cooling rack and allow harden.

6. Assemble salad in a large bowl by adding greens, blue cheese, candied pecans and dressing.

7. Toss gently before serving.

# sauces, dressings and marinades

# wild mushroom sauce

Prep time: 10 minutes / Cook time: 30 minutes / Yield: 3 cups

½ lbs fresh portabella mushrooms

½ lbs fresh shiitake mushrooms

½ lbs crimini mushrooms

2 tbsp salad oil

2 ½ tbsp  minced fresh ginger

3 ½ cups chicken or beef broth

1 tbsp cornstarch

salt and pepper to taste

1. Cut off and discard tough stems from mushrooms, rinse and drain caps.
2. Cut into ¼ wide strips
3. In a 10"-12" frying pan, combine mushrooms salad oil, and ginger.
4. Stir often on medium-high heat until mushrooms are lightly browned (*about 10 minutes*).
5. Pour broth into the pan.
6. Bring to a boil on high heat, stirring often, until sauce is reduced to about 2 ½ C (*15 to 20 minutes*).
7. Dissolve cornstarch with a little of the broth, stir into the pan.
8. Stir on high heat until boiling
9. Sauce will thicken lightly.

# chocolate sauce

Prep time: 5 minutes / Cook time: 10 minutes / Servings: 6

8oz semi-sweet chocolate or white chocolate

2 tbsp hot water

1 tbsp butter

1 egg yolk

½ cup heavy cream

1 egg white

1. In a double-boiler, place chocolate and stir in hot water.
2. Melt chocolate over boiling water.
3. Remove from heat.
4. Add butter, stir until melted.
5. Add egg yolk and heavy cream.
6. In a separate bowl beat the egg white until soft peaks form.
7. Fold into chocolate softly until incorporated.
8. Serve warm over favorite dessert.

# béchamel sauce

Prep time: 5 minutes / Cook time: 10 minutes / Yield: 2 cups

2 ½ cups milk

4 tbsp unsalted butter

3 tbsp all-purpose flour

¼ tsp salt

⅛ tsp fresh ground nutmeg

white pepper to taste

1. Heat milk to just below the boiling point, keep warm.

2. Melt butter in a heavy-based sauce pan over low heat.

3. Add flour and whisk to get rid of lumps.

4. Let the flour and butter paste heat through for approximately 2 minutes, stirring occasionally. *Do not let it brown.*

5. Add the hot milk in small increments, stirring constantly

6. Once all the milk has been added, simmer the sauce very gently for approximately 15 minutes, stirring constantly.

7. Add nutmeg, salt, and pepper toward the end of cooking.

*For cheese sauce add approximately ½ cup of your favorite cheese, i.e. Gruyere, fontina, mozzarella, freshly grated parmesan towards the end of cooking.*

# sweet and sour plum sauce                    ESS

Prep time: 5 minutes / Cook time: 10 minutes / Yield: 1 ½ cups

½ cup apple juice

¼ cup water

1 cup plum jelly

2 tbsp ketchup

1 tbsp cider vinegar

1. Place ingredients in a sauce pan over medium-high heat, stirring occasionally

2. Bring to a boil.

3. Serve warm.

# hot bacon **dressing**

Prep time: 10 minutes / Cook time: 5 minutes /Yield: ½ cup

4 slices of bacon

2 tbsp cider vinegar

2 tbsp water

1 tbsp sugar

1 egg, beaten

⅛ tsp pepper

1. Cook bacon in a large skillet until crisp.

2. Remove bacon and reserve drippings in the skillet.

3. Crumble bacon and set aside.

4. In the skillet, add vinegar, water and sugar to the drippings; Bring to a boil, remove from heat.

5. Add ¼ of the hot mixture into the beaten egg.

6. Add egg mixture to the skillet, stir constantly until well blended.

7. Cook over low heat stirring constantly until thickened.

8. Stir in bacon.

9. Immediately toss warm dressing over salad greens.

# pesto

Prep time: 10 minutes / Cook time: 0 minutes / Yield: 1 ¾ cups

2 cups basil

¼ cup grated parmesan cheese

½ cup pine nuts or walnut pieces

2 large garlic cloves cut in half

¼ tsp salt

¼ tsp fresh ground pepper

⅔ cup olive oil

1. Remove stems from basil.

2. Wash the leaves in warm water and drain well.

3. In a food processor, add basil, parmesan cheese, nuts, garlic, salt and pepper. Process until mixture is smooth

4. Continue processing adding the olive oil slowly until combined

# honey ginger **wine marinade**

Prep time: 10 minutes / Cook time: 2 minutes / Yield: 1 ½ cups

2 tbsp butter or margarine

1 cup dry white wine

2 tbsp white wine vinegar

⅓ cup honey

1 tsp finely chopped fresh mint or crumbled dry mint

2 cloves of garlic minced or pressed

1 tsp ginger fresh grater

½ tsp salt

¼ tsp pepper

1. In a sauce pan over medium heat melt the butter.
2. Remove from heat and stir in the remaining ingredients.

*great for chicken and pork*

# banana salsa

Prep time: 15 minutes / Cook time: 5 minutes / Yield: 1 cup

1 large firm ripe banana

1 tsp oriental sesame oil

1oz rum

½ cup chopped golden raisins

2 tbsp chopped cilantro

2 tbsp minced fresh lemongrass (tender part only) or 1 grated lemon zest

¼ tsp ground red pepper

½ tsp grated orange zest

½ tsp cinnamon

1. Peel and halve the banana lengthwise.
2. Brown the banana in a nonstick 10"-12" frying pan over high heat.
3. Add in oriental sesame oil (*about 8 minutes*).
4. Coarsely chop banana.
5. Mix with raisins, cilantro, lemongrass (or zest), ground pepper and orange zest.

*great for fish*

# red onion marmalade

Prep time: 15 minutes / Cook time: 45 minutes / Yield: 1 ¼ cups

2 tbsp olive oil

3 cups thinly sliced red onions (about 1 1/2 pounds)

¼ tsp dried crushed red pepper flakes

¼ cup (packed) dark brown sugar

¼ cup sugar

½ vanilla bean scraped

½ cup apple cider vinegar

¼ cup dry sherry

½ tbsp grated peeled fresh ginger

1 tsp coarse ground black pepper

¼ cup raisins

1. Heat oil in large heavy pot over medium heat.

2. Add onions and dried red pepper. Cover and cook until onions are tender, stirring occasionally (*about 15 minutes*).

3. Add brown sugar, sugar, vinegar, Sherry, vanilla, black pepper and ginger.

4. Cook uncovered until onions are tender and mixture is thick, stirring frequently (*about 15 minutes*).

5. Add raisins and cook until mixture is very thick and dark, stirring frequently (*about 12 minutes*).

6. Season to taste with salt and additional pepper if needed.

7. Cool completely and refrigerate.

 ote: *This recipe can be made up to 3 days ahead of time.*

# citrus mayonnaise

Prep time: 5 minutes / Cook time: 0 minutes / Yield: 1 ½ cups

1 ½ cups mayonnaise

4 tbsp lemon juice

1 tsp paprika

1 tsp dried thyme

1 tsp salt

1 tsp pepper

1 tsp grated orange rind

2 tbsp fresh orange juice

2 tsp fresh lime juice

½ tsp garlic

1. Stir together orange rind, orange juice, lime juice, garlic, and mayonnaise until blended.

2. Add the thyme and salt and pepper to taste.

3. Cover and chill at least 30 minutes

# spicy herb mustard **marinade**

Prep time: 10 minutes / Cook time: 0 minutes / Yield: 1 cup

½ cup dry white wines

⅔ cup olive oil

6 tsp champagne vinegar

2 tbsp finely chopped onion

1 tsp mixed Italian herbs

2 garlic cloves, minced

½ tsp ground pepper

¼ cup spicy brown mustard

½ tsp ancho chili powder

salt to taste

1. Combine all ingredients in a small bowl.
2. Make sure the meat is well covered and refrigerate overnight.

*great for chicken or pork*

# coffee cocoa **glaze**

Prep time: 5 minutes / Cook time: 2 minutes / Servings: 4

¼ cup butter, soften

⅓ cup coffee

¼ cup bottled steak sauce

1 tbsp unsweetened cocoa powder

1 tbsp brown sugar

1 tbsp honey

1. In a medium saucepan, simmer all ingredients over medium-high heat for approximately 1 minute or until sauce is thick and smooth.
2. Brush mixture over hot grilled meats during last 5 to 10 minutes of grill time.

# white chocolate orange **dressing**

Prep time: 10 minutes / Cook time: 5 minutes / Yield: 1 ½ cups

¼ cup champagne vinegar

⅓ cup reserved mandarin orange juice

¼ tsp salt

2 tbsp sugar

⅓ cup white chocolate chips

4 tbsp olive oil

1. Combine vinegar, mandarin juice, salt, and sugar in a small saucepan over medium-low heat.
2. Gently heat until sugar is dissolved.
3. Remove from heat and stir in white chocolate until melted
4. Set aside to cool (*Do not refrigerate*)
5. Before serving, slowly whisk in olive oil

# pepper aioli

Prep time: 15 minutes / cook time: 10 minutes / Yield: 2 cups

1 red pepper

2 egg yolks

2 cloves garlic

¼ cup red wine vinegar

1 to 2 tbsp cherry peppers, diced

salt to taste

1 ½ cup canola oil

1. Place red pepper on an open flame or grill. Turn on all sides. When fully charred, remove and cover with plastic wrap. Let pepper cool, until you can handle it comfortably.

2. Remove blackened skin to reveal the red color underneath. (*A paper towel will wipe off what you can't remove with your fingers*).

3. Coarsely chop the pepper and place in a food processor.

4. Add the egg yolks, garlic, vinegar, chili paste and salt to taste. Puree until the mixture is homogeneous.

5. While the machine is running, very slowly drizzle in the oil, until incorporated.

6. Check the aioli for texture and flavor. (*If it's too thick, add a few drops of water to thin it down; if it's too thin add more oil*).

7. The desired outcome is a fairly thin aioli.

8. Refrigerate until ready to use.

*Note: We suggest caution in consuming raw and lightly-cooked eggs due to the slight risk of Salmonella or other food-borne illness. To reduce this risk, we recommend you use only fresh, properly refrigerated, clean, grade A or AA eggs, and avoid contact between the yolks or whites and the shell.*

# sambal sauce

Prep time: 15 minutes / Cook time: 15 minutes / Yield: 1 ½ cups

1 cup chopped Serrano chilies, with seeds

2 tbsp white sugar

2 tbsp salt

1 tbsp belacan shrimp paste

1 tomato, chopped

½ onion, chopped

1 bulb garlic, peeled and crushed

2 tbsp fresh lime juice

2 tbsp vegetable oil

2 lemongrass, bruised

2 fresh curry leaves

1in galangal, thinly sliced

2 tbsp tamarind juice

1. Place Serrano, peppers, sugar, salt, shrimp paste, tomato, onion, garlic, and lime juice into a blender, and blend until smooth.

2. Heat vegetable oil in a saucepan over medium-high heat.

3. Stir in chili puree along with lemongrass, curry leaves and galangal.

4. Cook and stir until the mixture changes color and becomes very fragrant (*about 15 minutes*).

5. Stir in the tamarind juice, and cook for 1 minute more.

6. Strain before serving.

# sweet & spicy red pepper relish

serving/ ¾ cup of relish

1 red bell pepper chopped in small pieces

½ onion, chopped in small pieces

⅔ cup of sugar

½ cup of white vinegar

½ tsp of red pepper flakes (if you like less heat, use ¼ tsp. if you like more heat, add ¼ tsp.)

1. Add everything to a small sauce pan and stir all the ingredients until well incorporated.

2. Cook relish on medium heat for 25 minutes stirring occasionally. *Most of the liquid from the relish will reduce.*

3. Remove from heat and allow relish to cool before being served.

*This recipe is very versatile.  If you want some spice add some other pepper varieties with the ones listed in the recipe above.  The picture is a shot from my excursion to Spain.  The produce and meat markets are fabulous!!*

# blueberry vinaigrette

Prep time: 15 minutes / Cook time: 0 minutes / Yield: 2 cups

8oz blueberry puree

3oz champagne vinegar

juice from 1 lime

2oz walnuts

1 shallot

2oz parmesan cheese

4oz honey

24oz vegetable oil

salt to taste

pepper to taste

water

1. Place blueberry puree, champagne vinegar, lime juice, walnuts, shallot, parmesan cheese, and honey into a food processor and process until smooth.

2. With processor running add the oil in a slow steady stream to create an emulsion.

3. Strain the vinaigrette through a chinois and thin with water until desired thickness is reached.

# raspberry-grand marnier syrup                    ESS

Prep time: 5 minutes / Cook time: 5 minutes / Yield: 4 cups

5 tbsp melted butter

½ cup granulated sugar

2 pints fresh raspberries

dash of grand marnier

1. In a sauté pan, melt the butter. Add the sugar, stirring constantly until the sugar dissolves (*about 1 minute*).

2. Add the raspberries and sauté for 2 to 3 minutes.

3. Remove from heat and add the Grand Marnier.

4. Flame the liqueur and continue to cook for 1 minute.

*This is wonderful over chocolate pancakes or waffles*

# cranberry horseradish mayonnaise

Prep time: 5 minutes / Cook time: 5 minutes / Yield: 4 cups

1 cup mayonnaise

3 tbsp whole berry cranberry sauce

1 tbsp prepared horseradish,

salt and pepper to taste

1 tsp honey, if sweetness is desired

1. Mix together mayo, cranberry sauce, horseradish and lemon juice until well combined.

2. Add salt, pepper and honey. Mix well.

3. Cover and refrigerate until ready to use.

# boysenberry syrup

Prep time: 15 minutes / Cook time: 20 minutes / Yield: 4 cups

2 cups fresh boysenberries

3 cups water

2 whole cinnamon sticks

½ cup molasses

½ cup light brown sugar

1ea vanilla bean

1. Place boysenberries, water, cinnamon sticks and scraped vanilla bean in a small saucepan.

2. Cook over low heat for about 20 minutes.

3. Remove cinnamon sticks and strain.

4. Add molasses and sugar.

5. Let cool.

*Pour over pancakes, crepes or ice cream*

# blackberry syrup                                    ESS

Prep time: 10 minutes / Cook time: 15 minutes / Yield: 1 cup

3 cups fresh blackberries

¾ cups sugar

1 ½ tsp grated lemon peel

⅓ cup water

1 ea cinnamon stick

1. In heavy 3 quart saucepan, combine blackberries, sugar, lemon peel and water. Mix gently. Cook over medium heat, stirring constantly, until sugar dissolved.

2. Bring to boiling over medium high heat. Reduce heat. Simmer, uncovered, for 8 minutes, stirring occasionally, until fruit is soft.

3. White cooking 2 to 3 more minutes, gently mash fruit against pan with wooden spoon.

4. Cool to lukewarm. Strain fruit mixture by pressing through a sieve. Pour into a storage container.

5. Cover and refrigerate up to 2 weeks.

# hollandaise sauce

Prep time: 10 minutes / Cook time: 10 minutes / Yield: 2 cups

½ lb and 4 tbsp unsalted butter, cubed

4 egg yolks

1 tbsp cold water

2 tbsp lemon juice

¼ tsp white pepper

½ tsp salt

½ tsp Creole seasoning

1. In a skillet, melt the butter over medium heat and remove skillet once the butter is melted.

2. Whisk the egg yolks and water in a saucepan until foamy.

3. Place the egg yolk mixture over low heat until the mixture thickens. Do not let the eggs come to a boil or they will scramble.

4. Lift the egg mixture from the heat to cool from time to time.

5. Slowly ladle the butter into the eggs while whisking, until the sauce thickens.

6. Beat in the lemon juice, salt, pepper and Creole seasoning.

7. Serve on a delicious crab benedict or dish of your choice.

# tuscan marinade

Prep time: 15 minutes / Cook time: 0 minutes / Yield: 2½ cups

1 cup olive oil

6 tbsp lemon juice

¼ cup garlic, chopped

¼ cup thyme

¼ cup rosemary leaves. crushed

¼ cup basil leaves

1 tbsp black pepper, ground

1 tbsp salt

1. Combine all ingredients and whisk together

2. Use in the flat iron steak sandwich recipe or in your favorite grilled meat recipes.

# fresh pineapple chutney

Prep time: 10 minutes / Cook time: 20 minutes / Yield: 2 cups

1 ripe sweet pineapple

1 tbsp apple cider vinegar

2 tbsp sugar

¼ tsp cinnamon, ground

¼ tsp salt

1. Cut the pineapple in quarters and remove the cores off each quarter.

2. Cut the pineapple into bite-sized pieces, then in half.

3. Place all ingredients in a medium saucepan and bring to a simmer over medium heat (about 15 to 20 minutes).

4. Serve warm in the chicken curry salad wrap. Will stay fresh for up to 12 hours (covered and refrigerated).

# *sandwiches*

# ham and Swiss sandwich with blueberry chutney

Prep time: 15 minutes / Cook time: 5 minutes / Yield: 2 cups

*blueberry chutney*

2 cups fresh or frozen blueberries

½ cup minced onion

1t tbsp grated fresh ginger root

⅓ cup apple cider vinegar

½ cup brown sugar

½ cup dried blueberries

2 tbsp cornstarch

1 cinnamon stick

salt to taste

*sandwich*

12 slices rye bread

spicy brown or whole grain mustard

6 thin slices cooked ham

6 thin slices cooked turkey

6 thin slices of chicken

6 thin slices Swiss or American cheese

*blueberry chutney*

1. In a medium saucepan over medium heat, bring all ingredients to a boil, stirring frequently.

2. Boil 1 minute and remove cinnamon stick.

3. Cool completely

4. Place tightly in sealed containers, and refrigerate for up to 2 weeks.

*sandwich*

1. Spread each slice of bread with a thin amount of mustard.

2. Add a smear of blueberry chutney.

3. Layer the ham and cheese on the sandwich and top each one with the other slice of bread.

4. Serve and enjoy!

---

**Chutney**
**chut·ney** [ chútnee ] (*plural* chut·neys)

**Definition:**

1. **spicy relish:** a sweet and spicy relish made from fruit, spices, sugar, and vinegar.

2. *Caribbean* **rhythmic Caribbean song:** a popular Caribbean form of song with a quick beat, much influenced by calypso in rhythm and choice of subjects.

---

# french toasted **ham sandwich** with blueberry chutney

Prep time: 15 minutes / Cook time: 0 minutes / Servings: 6

12 slices rye bread

spicy brown or whole grain mustard

6 thin slices cooked ham

6 thin slices cooked turkey

6 thin slices of chicken

6 thin slices Swiss or American cheese

2 eggs, slightly beaten

½ cup milk

¼ tsp salt

½ tsp vanilla

black pepper, to taste

3 tbsp butter

blueberry chutney recipe pg 63

1. Spread each slice of bread with a thin amount of mustard.

2. Add a smear of blueberry chutney.

3. Layer the ham, turkey, chicken, and cheese on the sandwich and top each one with the other slice of prepared bread.

4. Combine eggs, milk, salt, and pepper. Melt butter in a skillet over low heat.

5. Dip sandwiches in the milk-egg mixture, turning to coat each side.

6. Brown in skillet.

 *Ham sandwiches are first assembled then dipped into an egg mixture then toasted or grilled.*

# chicken curry salad wrap

Prep time: 20 minutes / Cook time: 0 minutes / Servings: 4

2 tbsp olive oil

4 large tortillas or wraps

1 ½ pound skinless chicken breast, cooked cut into 1 inch cubes

salt

1 yellow onion, small dice

2 tbsp yellow curry powder

½ cup dark raisins

½ granny smith apple peeled, cored, and diced

½ golden delicious apple peeled, cored, and diced

½ cup chopped fresh cilantro (just lightly packed)

2 green onions, sliced

3 tbsp mayonnaise

½ cup pineapple chutney (see recipe in sauce section)

1. Mix together the mayonnaise, green onion, yellow onion, curry and powder. *This will make the dressing for the rest of the ingredients.*

2. Next add in pineapple chutney and mix well.

3. Add the dark raisins and mix to incorporate.

4. Add the diced chicken to the curry mixture.

5. Refrigerate until cool.

6. When you are ready to make the wraps, mix the apple, and cilantro into the chicken salad.

7. Place 1/4 of the salad in the middle of a wrap.

8. Fold the sides over the salad.

9. Fold the bottom flap over the salad.

10. Roll up the wrap starting at the bottom.

*The chicken curry salad can easily be made a day ahead.*

# grilled tuna sandwich with sweet and spicy red pepper relish on thyme focaccia

Prep time: 25 minutes / Cook time: 8 minutes / Servings: 6

2 pounds 1/2-inch-thick tuna steaks

2 tbsp fresh lemon juice

1 tsp minced fresh thyme leaves

¼ cup plus 2 tbsp extra-virgin olive oil

2 cups fresh flat-leafed parsley leaves

⅛ cup sliced red onion (about 1)

6 pieces of sandwich size focaccia

3 large red bell peppers, roasted and peeled

2 tbsp drained capers

1 recipe sweet and spicy red bell pepper relish (*see sauces, dressings and marmalades*)

1.  Prepare the grill by oiling the rack set 5-6 inches over the coals.

2.  Season tuna steaks with salt and pepper

3.  Grill tuna 3 to 4 minutes on each side, or until just cooked through.

4.  Transfer tuna to a platter and cool.

5.  In a large sealable plastic bag, combine lemon juice, thyme, parsley, capers, and 1/4 cup oil.

6.  Add grilled tuna.

7.  Marinate grilled tuna, chilled, turning bag occasionally, at least 1 hour and up to 1 day.

8.  Prepare the Sweet and Spicy Red Bell Pepper Relish

9.  Cut the focaccia in half horizontally

10. Spread the sweet and spicy red pepper relish on each half.

11. On the bottom layer assemble with peppers, tuna, and red onion.

12. Top sandwich with remaining focaccia half, pressing gently.

In some cases you can buy an entire small sheet of focaccia and cut them to your desired size.

# flat iron steak sandwich with onion marmalade

Prep time: 20 minutes / Cook time: 15 minutes / Servings: 4

4 tsp softened butter

2 tsp chopped garlic

2 tbsp vegetable oil

4 (4 ounce) thinly-cut flat iron steaks marinated in Tuscan marinade (see sauce section)

½ cup fresh spinach leaves

1 tomato, sliced

½ cup crumbled blue cheese

4 tsp whole grain mustard

2 tsp balsamic vinegar, for drizzling

4 sandwich rolls, partially split

1 cup red onion marmalade (*see sauces, dressings and marmalades*)

1. Preheat oven broiler on high heat.

2. In a bowl, mix the softened butter and garlic.

3. Open the sandwich rolls and spread each with about 1 tsp of garlic butter mixture.

4. Toast the sandwich rolls in the broiler about 5 minutes, until the edges are golden brown. Set aside.

5. Heat a large, heavy skillet over high heat, and add the vegetable oil.

6. Remove the flank steaks from the marinade and shake off excess marinade.

7. When oil just begins to smoke, drop in the flat iron steaks and quickly sear until steaks are browned (*about 3 to 4 minutes*).

8. Flip the steaks over and sear the other side for another 3 to 4 minutes.

9. Remove the steaks immediately. Set aside and keep warm.

10. Assemble spinach leaves and tomato on one side of the sandwich roll. Sprinkle with ½ tsp balsamic vinegar.

11. Spread red onion marmalade on the other half of the sandwich roll. Sprinkle with blue cheese. Top with steak.

12. Fold sandwich and serve.

# smoked turkey club sandwich with apple stuffing

Prep time: 10 minutes / Cook time: 10 minutes / Servings: 3

9 slices of honey wheat bread

½ cup cranberry mayonnaise

½ head Boston bibb lettuce

8 oz smoked turkey

1ea ripe tomato

6 strips bacon, cooked

1 cup apple stuffing (*see sides*)

1. For each sandwich, lightly toast and butter large slices of your favorite firm bakery honey wheat bread.

2. Spread cranberry horseradish mayonnaise on each slice of toast.

3. On the bottom slice, add a few slices of smoked turkey and apple stuffing.

4. Add second slice of toast and top with lettuce, tomato , and bacon.

5. Add the third slice of toast.

# grilled turkey reuben

Prep time: 10 minutes / Cook time: 8 minutes / Servings: 4

8 tsp thousand island salad dressing

8 slices rye bread

8 ounces cooked turkey, thinly sliced

1 ⅓ cup sauerkraut – drained

4 slices Swiss cheese

4 slices tomato, optional

4 tbsp butter

1. Heat griddle over medium heat.  Butter one side of each piece of rye bread.

2. Spread 1 tsp dressing on each of the slices of rye bread and place on the griddle.  Top each piece of rye bread with Swiss cheese.

3. Place the sliced turkey on the griddle next to the bread.   Spoon 1/3 cup sauerkraut on to the griddle next to the turkey.  Place a tomato slice on the griddle as you see the Swiss cheese starting to melt.

4. To assemble place a tomato slice on four out of eight slices of bread.  This is the base for your reubens

5. Next place the sauerkraut on the tomato and then top with the turkey.  Finish by placing the rye bread on top of each sandwich.  Enjoy.

# cherry chipotle **barbecue sauce**

Prep time: 5 minutes / Cook time: 20minutes / Servings: 8

1 cup fresh or frozen dark sweet cherries, pitted and chopped

½ cup reduced-sodium chicken broth

⅓ cup cherry preserves

⅓ cup ketchup

1 tbsp honey

2 tbsp cider vinegar

1 ½ tsp minced canned chipotle peppers

1 ¼ tsp dried thyme

½ tsp ground allspice

2 pounds boneless, skinless chicken breasts

16 slices sourdough bread

16 slices provolone cheese

32 slices bacon, cooked

1 head green leaf lettuce

16 slices of tomato

1. Stir cherries, broth, preserves, ketchup, vinegar, chipotle peppers, thyme and allspice in a small deep bowl.

2. Reserve half of the mixture and set aside.

3. Transfer the remaining half of the mixture into a glass dish large enough to hold chicken. (*Do not use a reactive dish; do not use a reactive metal pan or dish to hold the marinade and chicken*). Add the chicken and turn to coat well. *Recommend: Marinate in the refrigerator overnight.*

4. Place the remainder in a sauce pan on medium heat and cook until thickened.

5. Once thickened, place the mixture in a blender and puree. Add the honey and set aside.

6. Preheat grill to high. Oil the grill rack.

7. Remove the chicken from the marinade. (*You can save the marinade and reduce it like you did the mixture in the beginning*).

8. Reduce the grill heat to medium and grill the chicken until cooked. Let the chicken cool slightly.

9. Heat your Panini Grill to medium high heat.

10. Assemble the sandwich by spreading the cherry chipotle barbecue sauce on the pieces of sour dough.

11. Add the provolone, chicken, lettuce, 2 slices of tomato, 2 slices of bacon and top with provolone and a piece of sourdough that has been prepared with the cherry chipotle barbecue sauce.

 Highly acidic foods can react with certain types of pans. Make sure the pan you use for this recipe is non-reactive.

# grilled chicken sandwich with jicama slaw

Prep time: 20 minutes / Cook time: 10 minutes / Servings: 8

8 ciabatta rolls

2 pounds chicken breast (4 oz breasts), marinated in Tuscan (see sauces)

3 tbsp olive oil

2 granny smith apple, sliced

16 thin slices Munster cheese

1 recipe jicama slaw (*see sides*)

1 ½ cup citrus mayonnaise (*see sauces, dressings and marinades*)

1. Heat the skillet to medium high heat.  Add the olive oil.

2. While the skillet is heating, remove the chicken from the marinade and allow excess marinade to run off.

3. Cook chicken until done.  Reduce the heat to warm.

4. Cut rolls in half and spread citrus mayonnaise on each side of the rolls.

5. Add slices of Munster cheese and granny smith apple on the bottom bun of the roll.

6. Place the chicken on the sandwich and top with the jicama slaw. *Be sure to drain the slaw that you plan to put on your sandwich.*

7. Top with the other piece of the roll.

# *sides*

# glazed carrots

Prep time: 15 minutes / Cook time: 15 minutes / Servings: 6

1 pound baby carrots

water enough to cover carrots

½ cup honey

¼ cup maple syrup

1 tsp parsley

2 tbsp brown sugar

⅛ tsp nutmeg, ground

1 cinnamon stick

1. Fill a large sauce pan ¾ with water, bring to a boil.

2. Add carrots and cook until al dente.

3. Drain carrots, reserving 1 cup of liquid and set aside.

4. In the sauce pan add the reserved liquid,  a cinnamon stick, honey, maple syrup and brown sugar, bring to a simmer.

5. Add Nutmeg.

6. Return carrots to the pan stirring to cover with glaze and finish with parsley.

# pecan risotto with golden raisins

Prep time: 15 minutes / Cook time: 35 minutes / Servings: 4

5 cups vegetable or chicken stock

1 tbsp olive oil

2 ½ oz butter

1 small onion, finely chopped

1 ⅜ cups risotto rice

1 cup pecans

1 cup golden raisins

¾ cup freshly grated parmesan cheese

½ cup mascarpone cheese

2oz blue cheese, diced

pinch of ground nutmeg

salt and pepper

1. Bring the stock to a rolling boil in a pan, then reduce the heat and add the risotto.

2. Continue to simmer gently over low heat, cooking the risotto.

3. Heat the oil with two tablespoon of butter in a deep pan over medium heat until the butter has melted.

4. Add the onion and cook stirring occasionally (*5-7 minutes*), or until soft and turning golden. Do not brown.

5. Reduce the heat, add the rice and mix to coat.

6. Cook, stirring occasionally for 2-3 minutes, or until the rice is translucent.

7. Gradually add the hot stock one ladle at a time. Stirring constantly, adding stock as it is absorbed.

8. Increase the heat to medium so the liquid begins to boil.

9. Cook for 20 minutes, or until all the liquid is absorbed and the rice is creamy.

10. Salt and pepper to taste. Continue cooking the risotto.

11. Add 2 tablespoon of butter in a skillet over medium heat; add the pecans, golden raisins and raisins. Cook for 2-3 minutes.

12. Remove the risotto from the heat and add the remaining butter.

13. Mix well, and then stir in the parmesan, mascarpone and Gorgonzola until melted.

14. Serve immediately.

# wild mushroom risotto

Prep time: 15 minutes / Cook time: 30 minutes / Servings: 6

4 ½ cups chicken or vegetable stock

1lb combination of fresh wild mushrooms such as porcini, horse mushroom and chanterelles

4-6 oz black truffles brushed and clean

4 tbsp olive oil

3-4 garlic cloves finely chopped

3 oz butter

1 onion, finely chopped

1 ½ cup risotto rice

¼ cup dry white vermouth

1 cup freshly grated parmesan cheese

½ cup heavy cream

¼ cup truffle oil

4 tsp chopped fresh parsley

freshly grated nutmeg

salt and white pepper

1. Bring the stock to a boil in a sauce pan, then reduce the heat and add the risotto.

2. Simmer gently over low heat.

3. Brush the mushrooms and trim, cut larger mushrooms into small pieces.

4. In a large skillet heat 3 tablespoon of olive oil, add the garlic and the fresh mushrooms (*leaving the truffles for later use*).

5. Stir-fry for 2-3 minutes. Remove from pan and set aside.

6. In the same skillet, heat the remaining oil and half of the butter. Add the onion cook over medium heat stirring occasionally until softened.

7. Reduce the heat; add the rice, mixing until translucent.

8. Add the vermouth, stir constantly until reduced.

9. Gradually add the stock a ladle at a time as rice absorbs the liquid.

10. Increase the heat to medium letting the liquid bubble.

11. Cook for 20 minutes or until all the liquid is absorbed and rice is creamy.

12. Stir in the heavy cream. Season with a little nutmeg salt and white pepper. Continue cooking until the liquid is absorbed.

13. Remove the risotto from the heat; add the remaining butter, parmesan cheese and parsley.

14. After platting top serving with shave truffles and lightly drizzle with a little truffle oil.

15. Serve immediately.

# tesha's roasted red potatoes

Prep time: 15 minutes / Cook time: 30 minutes / Servings: 4

3 lbs small red new potatoes cut into quarters

¼ tbsp olive or vegetable oil

1 tsp salt

fresh ground pepper

1 tsp rosemary (dried)

½ tsp thyme (dried)

½ tsp basil (dried)

½ tsp parsley (dried)

¼ tsp garlic salt

2 ½ tsp minced onion (dried)

¼ tsp paprika

1 tsp minced garlic

1. Preheat oven to 400°F
2. In a bowl combine oil, salt, pepper, rosemary, thyme, basil, parsley, garlic salt and garlic. Mix well.
3. Add potatoes and toss until coated.
4. Pour potatoes on a medium sheet pan.
5. Bake for 30 minutes or until tender.
6. Transfer to a serving dish.

# brown rice pilaf

Prep time: 10 minutes / Cook time: 20 minutes / Servings: 4

2 cups vegetable, beef or chicken stock

1 cup brown rice

⅓ cup shredded carrot

¾ tsp snipped fresh thyme or ¼ tsp dried thyme

dash black pepper

¼ cup thinly sliced green-onions

1 tbsp chopped fresh parsley

salt to taste

1. Place stock in a medium saucepan. Bring to a boil.
2. Stir in mushrooms, uncooked rice, carrot, thyme and black pepper.
3. Return to boiling and reduce heat.
4. Simmer, covered for 12 minutes or until tender.
5. Remove from heat. Let stand, covered for 5 minutes.
6. Add the green onions and parsley; fluff with a fork.

# butternut squash risotto

Prep time: 20 minutes / Cook time: 35 minutes / Servings: 4

4 cups vegetable or chicken stock

1 tbsp olive oil

3 tbsp butter

1 small Vidalia onion; finely chopped

8 oz butternut squash

1 ⅜ cups (generous) risotto rice

⅔ cups dry white wine

1 tsp crumbled saffron threads (optional)

¾ cup freshly grated parmesan or cheese

salt and pepper to taste

1. Bring the stock to a boil. Reduce the heat and keep simmering gently over low heat while preparing the risotto.

2. Heat the oil with 2 tablespoon of the butter in a deep pan over medium heat until the butter has melted.

3. Stir in the onion and butternut squash and cook, stirring occasionally, for 5 minutes, or until the onion is soft and starting to turn golden and the butternut squash begins to color.

4. Reduce the heat, add the rice, and mix to coat in oil and butter.

5. Cook, stirring constantly, for 2-3 minutes, or until the rice is translucent.

6. Add the wine and cook, stirring constantly, for 1 minute until it has reduced.

7. If using the saffron threads, dissolve them in 4 tablespoon of the hot stock and add the liquid to the rice after the wine has been absorbed.

8. Cook, stirring constantly, until the liquid has been absorbed.

9. Gradually add the hot stock, a ladle a time.

10. Stir constantly and add more liquid as the rice absorbs each addition.

11. Increase the heat to medium so that the liquid bubbles.

12. Cook for 20 minutes, or until all the liquid is absorbed and the rice is creamy. Season to taste.

13. Remove the risotto from the head; add the remaining butter and Parmesan until melted.

14. Adjust the seasoning if necessary.

15. Serve immediately.

# asparagus and sun-dried tomato **risotto**

Prep time: 20 minutes / Cook time: 35 minutes / Servings: 4

4 cups vegetable or chicken stock

1 tbsp olive oil

3 tbsp butter

1 Vidalia onion; finely chopped

6 sun-dried tomatoes, thinly sliced

2 cloves garlic; finely chopped

1 ⅜ cups risotto rice

⅔ cup dry white wine

8 oz fresh asparagus spears, cooked

¾ cup freshly grated parmesan cheese

salt and pepper

thinly pared lemon rind, to garnish

*Note: If using sun-dried tomatoes in oil. Simply drain them well before slicing. Sun-dried tomatoes from a package must first be soaked in boiling water until they are soft.*

1. Bring the stock to a boil in a pan, then reduce the heat and keep simmering gently over low heat while you are cooking the risotto.

2. Heat the oil with 2 tablespoon of the butter in a saucepan over medium heat until the butter has melted.

3. Stir in the onion and sun-dried tomatoes, and cook, stirring occasionally until the onion is soft and starting to turn golden.

4. Reduce the heat, add the rice, and mix to coat in oil and butter.

5. Cook, stirring constantly, for 2-3 minutes, or until the grains are translucent.

6. Add the wine and cook, stirring constantly, until it has been reduced.

7. Gradually add the hot stock, a ladle at a time as the rice absorbs the liquid.

8. Increase the heat to medium so that the liquid bubbles.

9. Cook for 20 minutes, or until all the liquid is absorbed and the rice is creamy. Season to taste.

10. While the risotto is cooking, cut most of the asparagus into pieces about 1 inch/2.5 cm long. *Keeping several spears whole for garnishing the finished dish.*

11. Carefully fold the cut pieces of asparagus into the risotto for the last 5 minutes of cooking time.

12. Remove the risotto from the heat and add the remaining butter.

13. Mix well, stir in the Parmesan until melted.

14. Serve garnishing with whole spears of asparagus.

15. Sprinkle the lemon rind on top and serve.

# baby spinach with walnuts and raisins

Prep time: 5 minutes / Cook time: 10 minutes / Servings: 4

2 ½ lb baby spinach, washed and picked

6 oz butter

¼ lb raisins

¼ lb chopped walnuts

Salt and pepper to task

1. In a large skillet, melt butter, add spinach, and cook until it begins to wilt.

2. Add raisins and walnuts. Mix well.

3. Salt and pepper to taste.

# carrots and cabbage

Prep time: 10 minutes / Cook time: 15 minutes / Servings: 4

1 lb cabbage sliced

1 ½ lb sliced carrots

1 Vidalia onion; sliced

6 cups chicken or vegetable stock

4 oz butter

2 oz parsley chopped

salt and pepper to taste

1. In a stock pot, place the carrots in cold salted stock and bring to a boil. Cook until the carrots have a slight crunch.

2. Drain and place carrots in an ice water bath.

3. In a sauce pan, heat the butter. Sauté cabbage and onions until tender. Add the carrots.

4. Season with salt and pepper to taste.

5. Finish with parsley.

# chayote squash

Prep time: 10 minutes / Cook time: 10 minutes / Servings: 5

½ stick butter, unsalted

4 chayote squash

freshly ground nutmeg to taste

½ cup milk

salt and white pepper to taste

1. In a large skillet, melt butter over medium heat.

2. Add sliced squash, cooking over high.

3. Heat for approximately 2 minutes.

4. Add nutmeg and milk.

5. Cover and simmer approximately 4 minutes or until squash is tender.

6. Add salt and pepper to taste.

# snow peas with ginger

Prep time: 10 minutes / Cook time: 10 min / Servings: 10

1 ½ lb snow peas

2 oz peanut oil

2 oz ginger grated

½ tsp garlic

salt and pepper

1. Remove the ends of the snow peas and wash.

2. Blanch the snow peas in salted boiling water; then shock in ice water.

3. In a sauté pan, heat the oil, add the garlic and ginger.

4. Add the snow peas and toss until heated.

5. Season with salt and pepper to taste.

# sauté spinach with sarrachi and thai chili

Prep time: 10 minutes / Cook time: 5 minutes / Servings: 6

2 tbsp butter

1/4 cup chopped shallot (about 1 large)

1 tbsp minced peeled fresh ginger

2 garlic cloves, minced, divided

½ Serrano Chile, seeded, minced, divided

4 5-ounce bags baby spinach

coarse kosher salt

1 tsp sarrachi

1 tbsp sweet thai chili sauce

1. Melt 2 tablespoons butter in heavy large skillet over medium heat.

2. Add shallot, 1 tbsp ginger, 2 minced garlic cloves, and minced chile.

3. Sauté until shallot is soft (*about 2 minutes*).

4. Increase heat to medium-high and add 1 bag of spinach.

5. Stir until spinach begins to wilt.

6. Add remaining spinach, 1 bag at a time, stirring and wilting between additions.

7. Add sarrachi and sweet thai chili sauce.

8. Season with coarse salt and pepper.

9. Keep warm.

# asparagus with citrus buerre blanc

Prep time: 15 minutes / Cook time: 15 minutes / Servings: 6

1 oz white wine

1 ½ oz lemon juice

1 tsp orange zest

1 ½ oz lime juice

10 oz heavy cream

5 ⅓ oz un-salted butter

16 oz water

pinch of salt

1. Bring a medium pot of water to a boil. Add a pinch of salt. Reduce to a simmer.

2. Blanch the asparagus spears in the simmering water until done. (*Slightly crisp*).

3. Place the first three ingredients into a pot and put on a medium heat. Reduce the liquid by two thirds to concentrate the flavor.

4. Remove mixture from heat and whisk in 8 ounces of heavy cream and the orange zest.

5. Return the mixture to the heat and reduce by two thirds (*mixture will be almost a butter cream sauce consistency*).

6. Remove from the heat and whisk in the remaining heavy cream.

7. Stir in large pieces of soft butter.

8. Place asparagus on a plate and pour a small amount of sauce on the asparagus.

   NOTE:  All ingredients must be ready prior to starting this recipe.

# apple walnut cornbread stuffing

Prep time: 10 minutes / Cook time: 30 minutes / Servings: 3

2 cups fresh cornbread cubes

1 tsp olive oil

½ small onion, diced finely

1/3 cup chopped celery

½ medium granny smith apples, peeled and diced

3 tbsp cup chopped walnuts

3 tbsp cup minced fresh parsley

¼ tsp. dried ground sage

½ tsp. dried thyme

½ cups low-sodium chicken broth

¼ tsp salt

¼ tsp. pepper

1. Preheat oven to 350°F.

2. Spread the cornbread cubes on a sheet pan and toast in the oven until lightly browned (*8-10 minutes*).

3. Remove the cornbread cubes from oven and put in a large mixing bowl.

4. Heat olive oil in a large skillet over medium-high heat. Add onion and celery, stirring until onion is translucent.

5. Add apples to skillet and cook another 5 minutes.

6. Remove from the heat and pour over cornbread cubes.

7. Add the remaining ingredients to the mixing bowl, tossing well.

8. Put the mixture into a 9 x 13" baking pan coated with cooking spray. Bake, covered with aluminum foil, for 20 minutes.

9. Remove the aluminum foil and bake 10 more minutes. *Stuffing should be browned on the top.*

# sauté haricot verts with sugared almonds          ESS

Prep time: 15 minutes / Cook time: 15 minutes / Servings: 4

½ pound of haricot vert, trimmed and tailed

2 tsp butter

1 small shallot, sliced

salt and pepper to taste

2 tbsp diced tomato

wedge of lemon

1. Bring a pot of well-salted water to boil. Boil haricot vert for 2.5 minutes then put them into an ice bath. Drain the beans.

2. In your empty pot, melt two tbsp of butter over medium heat. Add the shallot and sauté them until they're just translucent.

3. Add the drained and cooled haricot vert and reheat them with the butter and shallots. Season with salt and pepper.

4. Spread haricot vert and shallot onto a plate, throw the diced tomato over them and squeeze a few drops of lemon juice over the dish.

5. Add the candied almonds and serve immediately.

# sugared almonds          ESS

Prep time: 15 minutes / Cook time: 1 hour / Servings: 3 cups

serving/3 cups

1 egg white

3 cups sliced almonds

⅓ cup sugar

salt to taste

1. Beat egg white until foamy, add sugar and almonds, tossing to coat. Sprinkle a little bit of salt to taste.

2. Spread almonds on a greased baking sheet in a single layer.

3. Bake at 250°F for 1 hour.

4. Cool slightly and break apart.

5. Cool completely and store in airtight container.

# herb roasted potatoes

Prep time: 10 minutes / Cook time: 55 minutes / Servings: 4

1 ½ pounds red or Yukon gold potatoes, peeled, cut into wedges

1 tbsp melted butter

1 tbsp vegetable oil

2 tbsp fresh chopped parsley

½ tsp dried dill weed

½ tsp fresh rosemary, minced

½ tsp onion powder

¼ tsp garlic powder

salt and pepper

1. Preheat oven to 375°F.

2. Line a baking sheet with foil; grease the foil lightly.

3. Combine potatoes, butter, oil, parsley, dill, rosemary, and onion and garlic powders in a bowl.   Mix well until potato wedges are thoroughly coated.

4. Arrange potatoes in the prepared baking pan in a single layer. Sprinkle with salt and pepper.

5. Bake for 45-55 minutes, or until potatoes are tender and nicely browned.

# jicama slaw

Prep time: 10 minutes / Cook time: 0 minutes / Servings: 8

1 large jicama, peeled and finely shredded

½ Napa cabbage, finely shredded

2 carrots, shredded

½ cup freshly squeezed lime juice

2 tbsp rice vinegar

2 tbsp ancho chili powder

2 tbsp honey

½ cup canola oil

salt and freshly ground black pepper

¼ cup finely chopped cilantro leaves

1. Place jicama, cabbage, and carrots in a large bowl.

2. Whisk together the lime juice, vinegar, ancho powder, honey, and oil in a medium bowl. Season with salt and pepper, to taste.

3. Pour the dressing over the jicama mixture and toss to coat well.

4. Fold in the cilantro.

5. Let stand at room temperature for 15 minutes before serving.

# dinner delights

# sweet and spicy wings

Prep time: 25 minutes / Cook time: 8 minutes / Servings: 4

5 lbs chicken wings

1 quart buttermilk

seasoning for chicken:

2 tbsp salt

2tbsp black pepper

2 tbsp dry mustard

4 tbsp paprika

2 tbsp ginger

1 tbsp garlic powder


*seasoning for sauce*

2 cups flour

2 tbsp celery seed

2 tbsp dry mustard

1 tbsp garlic powder

5 tsp thyme

1 tsp dried basil

1 tsp oregano

2 ea sticks of butter

1 lb brown sugar

2 cups hot sauce

1 tbsp black sesame seeds

½ cup sweet chili sauce

1. Soak the chicken wings in buttermilk overnight.

2. For the sauce, heat butter in a pan, as it begins to melt (*approximately halfway*) add the brown sugar and mix well. Stir constantly so it won't burn. *You want it to almost make a caramel.*

3. Add the hot sauce and continue to stir until incorporated.

4. Add sesame seeds and sweet chili.

5. Fry chicken wings until internal temperature is 165°.

6. Toss chicken in sauce and enjoy!

### Why We Soak the Chicken in Buttermilk

*Soaking the chicken in Buttermilk tenderizes the meat of the chicken through the use of protein enzymes activated that occur naturally in the buttermilk, which breakdown (tenderize)the cellular walls of the chicken meat itself. Similar to a common meat tenderizer you would use to tenderize a pot roast. The buttermilks natural flavor also imparts a unique taste to the chicken.  The Buttermilk also adds some natural sugars to the meat as it tenderizes.*

*The acids and sugars in buttermilk will give it a nice, tangy flavor.*

# cola glazed *pork tenderloin*

Prep time: 10 minutes / Cook time: 30 minutes / Servings: 4

3 lbs boneless pork tenderloin

1 tsp salt

1 tsp pepper

½ tbsp garlic

2 cups cola

for the sauce:

1 cup brown sugar

cola liquid reserved from pan

1 tbsp dry mustard

2 tbsp Dijon mustard

2 cups bread crumbs

1 cup demi-glace

1. Combine 2 cups of Cola and all remaining ingredients to form a paste. *You will use this paste to rub down the pork.*

2. Place pork in a pan and put remaining 2Cups of Cola in the pan.

3. Place the pork in the oven at 350°F and cook for 20 to 30 minutes. *The rub should start to caramelize. You can add more rub as desired. I normally add more at least twice. This makes a nice crust.*

4. Reserve cola liquid from the pan and strain with a mesh strainer.

5. Add liquid to 1 cup of demi-glace and reduce to a sauce consistency.

6. Serve pork loin sliced with cola sauce.

# miso sesame glazed **salmon**

Prep time: 15 minutes / Cook time: 8 minutes / Servings: 6

1 cup miso paste (soy bean paste)

1 cup low sodium soy sauce

½ cup brown sugar

2 tsp sesame oil

2 tsp chopped garlic

6 salmon fillets

1. In a large bowl combine the miso paste, soy sauce, sugar, sesame oil, and garlic.

2. Preheat grill to medium.

3. Brush salmon fillets with the glaze.

4. Grill over medium heat and continue applying glaze throughout the entire grilling process.

---

**What is Miso?**

***fermented soy product:*** *Japanese fermented soybean paste used mainly in vegetarian cooking*

---

# kennett square mushroom tart with mache salad and truffle vinaigrette

Prep time: 30 minutes / Cook time: 50 min / Yield: 1 tart

*olive oil tart dough*

9 oz light whole wheat flour or a 50 /50 mix of all purpose and whole wheat flour

1 tsp sea salt

1 tsp dried herbs (I use rosemary or thyme)

¼ cup olive oil

½ cup water

mache salad:

1 ea black truffle

cracked black pepper to taste

1 tbsp truffle vinaigrette

¼ cup olive oil

*tart filling*

2 lbs mixed mushroom (cremini, oyster, portabella)

salt to taste

pepper to taste

3 tbsp butter

3 shallots

½ tbsp chopped thyme

1 cup heavy cream

2 tbsp grated parmesan cheese

½ tbsp lemon juice

1 egg, well beaten

2 tbsp parsley

4 oz gorgonzola cheese

1 oz jack daniels

*olive oil tart*

1. Combine the flour, salt, and herbs on a mixer at a medium speed. Add the oil and continue to mix. Add the water and mix it until it until it is just mixed, then knead lightly by hand.

2. Turn the dough out onto a lightly floured work surface. Sprinkle a little flour on the dough and on the rolling pin. Roll the dough out into a circle large enough to fit your tart pan. *Add a little more flour underneath and on the dough when it seems on the verge of becoming sticky. Avoid overworking the dough.*

3. Transfer the dough carefully into the prepared pan and line it neatly. Trim the excess dough. Place the pan in the fridge for 30 minutes to rest.

4. Blind-bake the crust. Bake 20 to 25 minutes at 400°F until done.

5. Cool tart shells

*tart filling*

1. Heat pan over high heat and sauté mushrooms, salt, pepper,

2. Cook mushrooms down to half their value and add shallots, garlic, Jack Daniels and thyme and cook till light brown.

3. Add cream and reduce cream by about half

4. Stir in parmesan, gorgonzola, and lemon juice.

5. Turn off heat and quickly stir in beaten egg and cool at room temperature.

*complete*

1. Fill tart shell with filling and top with gorgonzola

2. Bake for 20 to 30 minutes at 350 F

3. Top with Mache salad and truffle vinaigrette

*Note: Make sure to grease your pan if it does not have a non-stick coating.*

# saffron and lemon risotto with scallops

Prep time: 25 minutes / Cook time: 35 minutes / Servings: 4

16 live scallops, shucked

juice of 1 lemon, plus extra for seasoning

5 cups fish or vegetable stock

1 tbsp olive oil, plus extra for brushing

3 tbsp butter

1 small onion, finely chopped

generous 1 ⅜ cups risotto rice

1 tsp crumbled saffron threads

2 tbsp vegetable oil

1 cup freshly grated parmesan or grana padano cheese

salt and pepper

*to garnish*

1 lemon, cut into wedges

2 tsp grated lemon zest

1. Place the scallops in a non-metallic bowl and mix with the lemon juice.

2. Cover the bowl with plastic wrap and let chill in the refrigerator for 15 minutes.

3. Bring the stock to a boil in a pan, then reduce the heat and keep simmering gently over low heat while you are cooking the risotto.

4. Heat the oil with 2 tbsp of the butter in a deep pan over medium heat until the butter has melted. Add the onion and cook, stirring occasionally, for 5 minutes, or until soft and starting to turn golden. *Do not brown.*

5. Add the rice and mix to coat in oil and butter. Cook, stirring constantly, for 2-3 minutes, or until the grains are translucent.

6. Dissolve the saffron in 4 tbsp of hot stock and add to the rice.

7. Gradually add the remaining stock, a ladleful at a time. Stir constantly and add more liquid as the rice absorbs each addition.

8. Increase the heat to medium so that the liquid bubbles. Cook for 20 minutes, or until all the liquid is absorbed and the rice is creamy. Season to taste.

9. When the risotto is nearly cooked, preheat a grill pan over high heat. Brush the scallops with oil and sear on the grill plan for 3-4 minutes on each side, depending on their thickness. *Take care not to overcook or they will be rubbery.*

10. Remove the risotto from the heat and add the remaining butter. Mix well then stir in the Parmesan until it melts. Season with lemon juice, adding just 1 tsp a time and tasting as you go.

11. Place a large scoop of risotto on each of 4 warmed plates. Arrange 4 scallops and lemon wedges around it, sprinkle with lemon zest, and serve at once.

*If you have to use frozen scallops, make sure that they are completely thawed before beginning.*

# lobster pizza with baby shrimp and smoked gouda

Prep time: 1 ½ hour / Cook time: 12 minutes / Servings: 4

*crust*

2 tsp granulated sugar

¾ tsp sea salt

2 tbsp olive oil

2 tsp active dry yeast

1 cup water

2 ½ cups all-purpose flour

*topping*

garlic olive oil to brush on crust

3 to 4 ripe tomatoes, thinly sliced

8-ounces cooked maine lobster meat, cut into bite-sized pieces

1 cup roasted corn

1 ea onion, diced

1 cup red potato, small dice

1 ea green bell pepper, brunoise

1 bunch basil leaves, sliced into thin strips (chiffonade)

8-ounces fresh smoked gouda cheese, thinly sliced, or 8-ounces goat cheese at room temperature

2-ounces freshly grated parmesan reggiano cheese

freshly ground pepper to taste

*note: if you are in a hurry purchase 1lb pizza dough from the supermarket or local bakery.*

1. Prepare crust in a mixer by dissolving yeast in the water. Add sugar, salt and oil. Mix on low speed to incorporate.

2. Add in the flour and knead until smooth. Stop the mixer and let the dough rest in the bowl. Cover the dough with plastic to prevent the dough from crusting. Let the dough rise until it has doubled in volume (*about 1 hour*).

3. Divide the dough into four pieces. On a lightly floured surface, roll each piece out into a circle.

4. Let the dough rest for a few minutes, then go back and roll each piece into an 8- to 10-inch circle. *Don't worry if they aren't perfectly round. They look better when they are not perfect. It looks more rustic.*

5. Place the dough on a waxed paper on a sheet pan.

6. Preheat one half of the grill to medium-high, and keep the other side at a low temperature. Brush the dough with olive oil.

7. Bring the prepared pizza dough and a tray with the topping ingredients to the grill.

8. Cook one piece of dough on the hot side of the grill. The dough will puff slightly. When the grill side of the dough becomes firm and striped with grill marks flip it over to the cool side of the grill. *This process generally takes 3 to 5 minutes depending upon the grill.*

9. Next, arrange the thinly sliced tomatoes on the crust, then the corn, peppers, lobster, and potatoes.

10. Sprinkle the top with the fresh basil.

11. Arrange the smoked gouda cheese over the top of the pizza, season with fresh pepper, and drizzle with olive oil.

12. Lower the grill lid and cook the pizza until the cheese is bubbly.

13. Repeat the process for the remaining pizzas.

14. Cut into wedges and serve.

*Crust can be made in a bread machine: Add ingredients to the bowl of your bread machine and set on the dough cycle.*

# open faced **lobster ravioli** with shrimp, swordfish, scallops and pink lobster sauce

Prep time: 1 hour / Cook time: 1 hour / Servings: 4

2 - 1 pound lobsters (live)

1 ea carrot, sliced

1 ea celery stalk, sliced

1 ea onion, large dice

old bay to taste (pinch)

2 tbsp olive oil

1 ⅓ cup finely chopped shallots

3 large garlic cloves, chopped

¼ cup Madeira

4 tsp tomato paste

3 cups chicken stock or canned low-salt broth

1 tbsp butter, room temperature

1 tbsp all purpose flour

½ cup whipping cream

⅓ cup lentils

2 tbsp butter

2 medium leeks (white and pale green parts only), thinly sliced

4 ounces shrimp

4 ounces swordfish

4 oz sea scallops

3 lasagna noodles

2 tbsp chopped fresh cilantro

## for the sauce

1.  Boil lobsters in pot of seasoned boiling water for approximately 8 minutes. *I generally like to season my water with lemon juice, pinch of old bay, carrot, celery and onion.*

2.  Transfer lobsters to bowl of ice water; cool and drain.

3.  Working over a large bowl to collect juices, break down the lobster removing claws, tails and cutting the body in half.

4.  Cut the tails in 2 inch pieces and remove the meat.

5.  Remove the meat from the claws and body.

6.  Transfer shells and bodies to the bowl with the juices.

7.  Slice meat; place in small bowl. Chill.

8.  Heat oil in large pan over medium-high heat. Sauté the shallots and garlic then add the Madeira to deglaze the pan. Add the tomato paste and bring to boil. Add the chicken stock, lobster shells and any juices; bring to boil. Reduce heat; simmer until reduced to 2 ½ cups, about 30 minutes.

9.  Strain liquid into saucepan. Make sure to press on the shells to get all of the juices. Mix butter and flour in bowl and add to lobster stock (liquid from above). Bring to a boil and whisk often to avoid scorching. Add cream and simmer the sauce until reduced to sauce consistency.

## for the filling

1.  Cook the lentils in medium saucepan of simmering water until tender. Drain the lentils. Melt butter in large pan over medium heat. Add leeks; sauté until tender, about 15 minutes. Add lentils, lobster meat, scallops, shrimp, swordfish and 1/2 cup lobster sauce. Mix and reserve as the filling.

2.  Cook pasta in pot of boiling salted water until just tender.

3.  Drain. Cut each noodle crosswise into 4 pieces. Divide the pasta among 4 shallow bowls. Rewarm filling, mix in cilantro and spoon over pasta. Bring sauce to simmer. Spoon over pasta. Top with a sprig of cilantro.

# espresso rubbed **beef tenderloin**

Prep time: 5 minutes / Cook time: 30 minutes / Servings: 6

2 pounds beef tenderloin, trimmed of fat and silver skin

*spice rub*

¼ cup finely ground coffee beans

½ cup brown sugar

¼ cup cocoa powder

1 tbsp chili powder

1 tbsp paprika

*sauce*

1 cup apple juice

2 tbsp cornstarch

1 can beef broth

3 tbsp butter

1. Remove meat from refrigerator 1 hour before roasting.

2. Preheat oven to 500°F.

3. In a small bowl, combine spice rub ingredients.

4. Rub meat generously with the spice mixture. Allow the meat to rest for 15 minutes and apply the rub again.

5. Place meat on a rack in a roasting pan. *Do not cover the meat.*

6. Place the meat in the oven, turn temperature down to 400°F and roast for 30 to 40 minutes, or until internal temperature of roast is 135°F for medium rare to 145°F for medium.

7. Remove from the oven; let meat rest for 10 minutes before slicing. *This is important or else the juices from the tenderloin will run out of the meat making it dry.*

8. Strain the juices from the pan into a sauce pan. Place the pan on the stove and bring to a boil. Add 1 can beef broth and return to a boil.

9. Combine cornstarch and apple juice to form a thin cornstarch mixture. Add this to the sauce pan and stir continuously for 3 minutes at high heat.

10. Reduce the heat to warm and whisk in 1 tbsp of butter at a time.

11. Slice meat and arrange on a platter.

12. Ladle a small amount of sauce over the beef.

# *desserts*

# rosewater **crème brûlée**

Prep time: 15 minutes / Cook time: 35 minutes / Servings: 10

5 cups heavy cream

½ cup + 2tbsp sugar

2 ½ pinches of salt

2 ½ tsp vanilla extract

8 egg yolks

1 ½ tbsp rosewater

1. Preheat Oven to 300°F.

2. Line the bottom of a large baking pan with a damp kitchen cloth.

3. Bring a large pot of water to boil.

4. While water is boiling, combine sour cream, ¼ cup sugar and salt in a saucepan over medium heat. Stir occasionally until steam rises (*4 to 5 minutes*).

5. In a medium bowl, beat egg yolks and vanilla until smooth.

6. Pour hot cream into yolks, a little at a time, stirring constantly, until cream is incorporated.

7. Pour mixture into four 6 oz. ramekins.

8. Place ramekins on the damp towel in the baking dish, and place the dish in the oven.

9. Pour boiling water into the baking dish to halfway up the sides of the ramekins.

10. Cover whole pan loosely with foil.

11. Bake 25 to 30 minutes, until the custard is just set.

12. Chill the ramekins in the refrigerator 4 to 6 hours.

13. Before serving, sprinkle 1 tbsp sugar over each custard.

14. Use a kitchen torch or oven broiler (*2 to 3 minutes*) to brown the tops.

*Rose Water*

*Definition:*
**water scented by rose petals:** *a fragrant liquid made by distilling or steeping rose petals in water.*

# lemon curd

Prep time: 10 minutes / Cook time: 15 minutes / Yield: 8 mini tarts

3 eggs

1 cup sugar

½ cup fresh lemon juices

¼ cup butter or margarine, melted

3 tbsp grated lemon peel

1. In the top of a double broiler, beat eggs and sugar.

2. Stir in lemon juice and lemon peel.

3. Cook over simmering water for 15 minutes or until thickened.

*Curd*

*curd* [ kurd ]

*Definition:*

*1. solid part of sour milk:* *the solid substance formed when milk coagulates. Use: for making cheese.*

*2. substance like milk curd:* *a food substance with a consistency similar to milk curd*

# almond lace **cookies**

Prep time: 20 minutes / Cook time: 10 minutes / Yield: 2 dozen

1lb butter

1lb sugar

1lb flour

1lb corn syrup

1lb almonds, sliced

1. Preheat oven to 350°F.

2. Prepare cookie sheets by covering with parchment or a silpat.

3. Cream the butter and sugar together in a mixer. Add flour and continue to mix.

4. Add the corn syrup and continue mixing.

5. Add the almonds and mix until incorporated.

6. Drop almond lace by the tbsp onto the parchment paper, no more than 3 per ½ sheet pan.

7. Bake for 10 minutes or until golden brown.

8. Remove from the oven

9. Let cool for 60-90 seconds.

10. Remove from the sheet pan and mold over a wooden rolling pin.

11. Let cool until firm.

# creamy rice pudding

Prep time: 10 minutes / Cook time: 25 minutes / Servings: 6

¾ cup uncooked white rice

2 cups milk. divided

1/3 cup sugar

¼ tsp salt

1 egg

2/3 cups golden raisins

1 tbsp butter

½ tsp vanilla extract

1 ea orange zest and juiced

2 ea star anise

1 ea cinnamon stick

1. In a medium saucepan, bring 1 ½ cups of water to a boil.

2. Add rice and stir. Reduce heat and cover. Simmer for 20 minutes.

3. After rice is cooked, combine 1½ cups cooked rice, 1½ cups milk, sugar, salt, *anise*, orange juice, orange zest and cinnamon stick in another saucepan.

4. Cook over medium heat until thick and creamy (*15 to 20 minutes*).

5. Stir in remaining ½ cup milk, beaten egg and raisins.

6. Cook 2 more minutes, stirring constantly.

7. Remove from heat, and stir in butter and vanilla.

8. Serve warm.

---

*Anise*

**an·ise** [ *ánniss* ]
**Definition:**
*food*

1. *Same as  aniseed*
2. **plant with licorice-flavored seeds:** *an aromatic plant with licorice-flavored seeds aniseed. Use: medicines, flavoring for food and drinks. Native to: Mediterranean.  Latin name Pimpinella anisum.*

# chocolate molten cake with vanilla bean ice cream

Prep time: 25 minutes / Cook time: 12 minutes / Yield: 1 cake

6 oz  chocolate, cut into ¼ inch pieces

10 tbsp unsalted butter, cut into 10 pieces

3 large eggs

3 large egg yolks

2/3 cup sugar

½  cup all-purpose flour

1 ea batch crème anglaise

1.  Set rack in the middle of the oven and preheat to 400°F.

2.  Half-fill a sauce pan with water and bring it to a boil. Turn off heat.

3.  Combine the chocolate and butter in a heatproof bowl and place over the hot water. Stir occasionally until melted.

4.  Whisk eggs and egg yolks together by hand in the bowl of an electric mixer.

5.  Whisk in the sugar and then butter and the chocolate mixture.

6.  Place the bowl on the mixer and mix on medium speed with the paddle for I minute.

7.  Remove the bowl and whisk in the flour by hand.

8.  Fill the mold to within ¼ inch (6mm) of the top.

9.  Bake for 10 to 12 minutes (*unmold one to see how liquid it is*), and then unmold onto warm dessert plates.

10. Serve with ice cream.

# texas sheet cake

Prep time: 15 minutes / Cook time: 25 minutes / Yield: 1 sheet cake

2 cups sugar

2 cups flour

½ tsp salt

2 sticks of margarine

1 cup water

2 tbsp cocoa

2 eggs

1tsp baking soda

1 tbsp vinegar

½ cup sour cream

1. Mix sugar, flour and salt in a medium bowl.
2. In a separate bowl, beat together eggs, baking soda, vinegar and sour cream.
3. Add butter, water, cocoa, and egg mixture to the medium bowl.
4. Bake in greased 11x17" cookie sheet at 375°F for 20 to 25 minutes.

# frosting for texas sheet cake

Prep time: 5 minutes / Cook time: 10 minutes / Yield: 1 sheet cake

1 stick of oleo

6tbsp milk

1tsp vanilla

4tbsp cocoa

1lb sugar

1. In a saucepan, bring oleo and milk to a boil.
2. Add vanilla, cocoa, and sugar.
3. Beat until smooth
4. Pour over the cake and spread.

# piña colada dip

Prep time: 5 minutes / Cook time: 0 minutes / Yield: 1 ½ cups

12oz pineapple tidbits

2oz sugar

1 cup sour cream

3oz pina colada mix

1 oz rum

1. Mix all ingredients in a bowl.
2. Refrigerate and Serve.

# caramelized banana split

Prep time: 5 minutes / Cook time: 5 minutes / Servings: 1

1 banana

2oz sugar

3 scoops vanilla ice cream

1oz caramel sauce

1oz chocolate sauce

1oz raspberry sauce

2oz whipped cream

1oz chopped hazelnuts

strawberries

maraschino cherry

almond lace cookie shell(*see recipe*)

gas-torch or oven broiler can be used (450 degrees)

1. Using the caramel, chocolate and raspberry sauces garnish a 12" plate using zig zag pattern.
2. Next put a dollop of whipped cream in the center of the plate and set the almond lace shell in the center of the plate using the whipped cream to support the shell.
3. Place 3 scoops of the vanilla in the shell.
4. Cut the banana lengthwise and lay on a sheet pan.
5. Sprinkle sugar over the banana to coat. Use a torch to caramelize the sugar and allow banana to cool. *Sugar will be hot.*
6. Once cooled enough to handle, place bananas on top of the ice cream with caramelized part of the banana facing upward.
7. Top with whipped cream and garnish chocolate sauce and maraschino cherry.
8. Last sprinkle chopped hazelnuts and cut strawberries on the plate.

# peach cobbler

Prep time: 30 minutes / Cook time: 30 minutes / Servings: 10 to 12

½ cup butter

1 c flour

1 ½ tsp baking powder

½ tsp salt

1 cup sugar

1 cup milk

3 cups peaches, peeled and sliced

2oz peach schnapps

1oz cinnamon schnapps

¼ tsp nutmeg

1. Preheat oven to 350 F

2. Put the butter in a 9X13 inch Pyrex baking dish and put the dish in the preheating oven.

3. While the butter is melting, mix up the batter by combining the flour, baking powder, salt, sugar and milk.

4. Cook peaches quickly with peach and cinnamon schnapps until alcohol cooks out. Add nutmeg.

5. When the butter is completely melted, remove the pan and pour the batter into the melted butter.

6. Carefully spoon the peaches and juice evenly over the batter.

7. Return the dish to the oven and bake for 30 minutes.

8. As the cobbler cooks, the batter will rise up and around the peaches.

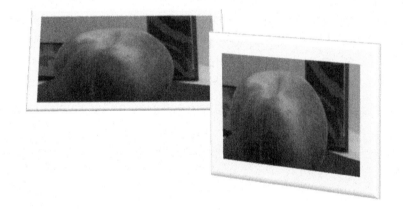

# grandma's sugar cookies

Prep time: 20 minutes / Cook time: 15 minutes / Yield: 6 dozen

2 cups butter

4 cups sugar

4 using tbsp heavy cream

4 tsp vanilla

½ tsp salt

4 tsp baking powder

8 cups flour

4 eggs

1. Cream butter and sugar in a mixer.  Add vanilla extract.
2. Slowly add eggs one at a time while mixing.  *You want each egg to be incorporated before you add another.*
3. Mix in heavy cream.
4. In a bowl mix together salt, baking powder and flour.
5. Add the dry ingredients to the wet ingredients on a slow to medium speed until incorporated.
6. Flip the mixture out onto a lightly floured surface and make a ball.
7. Wrap the dough and chill in the refrigerator for at least an hour.
8. To bake cookies, preheat oven to 350°F.
9. Take cookie dough from the refrigerator and cut off a small piece. Lightly work the piece you are able to roll the dough on a lightly floured surface.
10. Cut to the desired shape.
11. Bake for approximately 15 minutes.

# sugar cookie icing

1 cup & 3 tbsp confectioners' sugar

3 tbsp milk

2 tbsp light corn syrup

¼ tsp almond extract or clear vanilla

assorted food coloring

1. In a small bowl, stir together confectioners' sugar and milk until smooth.
2. Beat in corn syrup and almond extract until icing is smooth.  *The icing should appear glossy. If icing is too thick, add a little more corn syrup.*
3. Divide into separate bowls, and add food coloring to each to desired intensity.
4. Dip cookies, or paint them with a brush.

# sweet corn ice cream

Prep time: 7 hours / Cook time: 1 hour / Yield: 1 quart

4 ears fresh corn, shucked

2 cups milk

2 cups heavy cream

¾ cup sugar

9 large egg yolks

½ cup pure maple syrup

pinch of salt

1. Slice the kernels off the corn cobs and place them in a large saucepan. Break the corn cobs into thirds and add them to the pot as well.

2. Add the milk, heavy cream, and 1/2 cup of the sugar. Bring to a boil, and then turn off the heat.

3. Remove the cobs and puree the corn kernels.

4. Let stand for 1 hour. *This will allow the milk mixture to infuse with the corn flavor.*

5. Strain the mixture with a fine sieve, pushing down on the corn to get the entire flavor.

6. Bring the mixture back to a simmer.

7. In a small bowl, whisk the egg yolks and remaining 1/4 cup of sugar.

8. Add a cup of the hot cream to the yolks, stirring constantly so they don't curdle. *This is called tempering.*

9. Add the yolk mixture to the saucepan, stirring constantly with a heat proof spatula.

10. Add the maple syrup and pinch of salt.

11. Cook over medium-low heat, stirring constantly, until the custard thickens enough to coat the heat proof spatula (*about 10 minutes*).

12. Pass the custard through a fine sieve.

13. Let the custard cool, then cover and chill for at least 4 hours.

14. Freeze in an ice cream maker according to the manufacturer's directions.

# crème fraîche ice cream

Prep time: 6 hours / Cook time: 0 minutes / Yield: 1 quart

1 pound (about 2 cups) crème fraîche

2 cups buttermilk

⅓ cup fresh lemon juice

1 ¼ cups sugar

pinch of nutmeg

1. Combine all ingredients in a blender. Crape the sides well to make sure everything is incorporated.

2. Chill the mixture for about 2 hours

3. Place the mixture in an ice cream machine and follow the directions for the ice cream machine.

# chocolate caramel peanut butter cheesecake with bacon

Prep time: 20 minutes / Cook time: 1 hour 20 minutes / Servings: 12

6 pieces of bacon crumbled

1 container caramel apple dip

3 lb cream cheese

2 cups sugar

¼ cup peanut butter

½ cup melted chocolate

1 tbsp vanilla extract

1 tsp almond extract

for crust

2 cups graham cracker

½ cup sugar

1 stick butter

1. Pre heat oven to 350°F.

2. Combine 2 cups graham cracker crumbs, ½ cup sugar, and melted butter and mix thoroughly. Pour mixture in the bottom of a 10 inch spring form pan and pat firmly and evenly in the bottom. *I generally like to wrap my spring form pans at the bottom with aluminum foil to ensure they will not leak.*

3. In a food processor, blend the cream cheese, 2 cups of sugar, peanut butter and vanilla and almond extract, until smooth.

4. Add the eggs one at a time.

5. Once combined, add the melted chocolate until well incorporated.

6. Pour the cheesecake batter into the spring form pan.

7. Place the pan in another larger pan. *You want to create a water bath so that your cheesecake will bake slowly and evenly.* Fill the larger pan with water and bake for 1 hour and 20 minutes until done.

8. One finished, allow the cheesecake to cool and put in the refrigerator.

9. Once chilled and unmolded top with caramel and bacon bits.

# salted caramel ice cream

Prep time: 9.5 hours / Cook time: 30 minutes / Yield: 1 quart

2 cups whole milk, divided

1½ cups sugar

4 tbsp salted butter

½ tsp sea salt

1 cups heavy cream

5 large egg yolks

¾ tsp vanilla extract

1. To make the ice cream, you will need an ice bath. Fill a large bowl about a third full with ice cubes and add a cup or so of water. *You want to make sure the ice cubes are floating and that there is water and ice touching the bowl on top. The water and ice touching circulates the cold temperature evenly around the bowl.*

2. Nest a smaller metal bowl (at least 2 quarts/liters) over the ice. Pour 1 cup of milk into the inner bowl. Sit a fine strainer on top.

3. Put 1½ cups of sugar in a saucepan. *Make it an even layer so it cooks evenly.* Cook over medium heat, until caramelized. *You want to smell a hint a smoke but not burnt. It will be a golden color.*

4. Once caramelized, remove from the heat and stir in the butter and salt. Once the butter is melted, whisk in the cream, adding a little at a time. Continue to stir. *At times, the caramel may harden, but return it to the heat and stir over low heat until any hard caramel is melted.* Next stir in 1 cup of milk.

5. Whisk the yolks in a small bowl and slowly pour some of the warm caramel mixture over the yolks, stirring constantly. *This is an example of tempering. You want to do it gradually so you won't scramble the eggs.*

6. Scrape the warmed yolks back into the saucepan and cook the mixture using a heatproof utensil, stirring constantly. *You must scrape the bottom. This is the exact same technique used for crème anglaise and other cooked custards.* Stir until the mixture thickens and will coat the spatula.

7. Pour the custard through the strainer that you set up earlier and into the milk set over the ice bath.

8. Add the vanilla, and stir until the mixture is cooled down.

9. Refrigerate at least 8 hours or until thoroughly chilled.

10. Pour into an ice cream machine and follow the manufacturer's instructions.

# caramel sweet potato cheesecake

Prep time: 20 minutes / Cook time: 1 hour 20 minutes / Servings: 12

1 container caramel apple dip

1 lb  sweet potato, cooked

3 lb cream cheese

2 cups sugar

1 tbsp cinnamon

½ tsp nutmeg

½ tsp ginger

1 tbsp vanilla extract

1 tsp almond extract

for crust

2 cups graham cracker

½ cup sugar

1 stick butter

1. Pre heat oven to 350°F.

2. Combine 2 cups graham cracker crumbs, ½ cup sugar, and melted butter and mix thoroughly.

3. Pour the mixture into the bottom of a 10 inch spring form pan and pat firmly and evenly in the bottom. *I generally like to wrap my spring form pans at the bottom with aluminum foil to ensure they will not leak.*

4. In a food processor, blend the cream cheese, 2 cups sugar, vanilla and almond extract, and spices until smooth.

5. Mix in the eggs one at a time.

6. Once combined, add the sweet potatoes until well incorporated.

7. Pour the cheesecake batter into the spring form pan.

8. Place the pan in another larger pan. Fill the larger pan with water (*You want to create a water bath so that your cheesecake will bake slowly and evenly*). Bake for 1 hour and 20 minutes until done.

9. Cool the cheesecake in the refrigerator.

10. Once chilled, top with caramel.

# champagne sorbet

Prep time: 6.5 hours / Cook time: 0 minutes / Servings: 1 quart

1 ½  cups sparkling wine or champagne

1 cup white granulated sugar

1 tbsp light corn syrup

1 tsp of lemon and or grapefruit zest

1 ½  cups fresh grapefruit juice

¼ cup fresh squeezed lemon juice (meyer if you have access to them)

1 bottle champagne

1. Put champagne, sugar, corn syrup, and zest into a saucepan.

2. Bring to a vigorous boil so that the sugar completely dissolves, remove from heat.

3. Strain into a stainless steel bowl; add the grapefruit juice and lemon juice.

4. Chill completely.

5. Process the mixture in your ice cream maker according to the manufacturer's directions.

6.  Transfer mixture to a storage container and freezer in your freezer until firm, at least 6 hours.

7. Once frozen, enjoy with your favorite champagne and some grapes or strawberries.

# beverages and cordials

# bloody mary

Servings: 2

wedge lemon

Worcestershire sauce to taste

fresh lemon juice to taste

1 tbsp kosher salt

2 tsp celery salt

3oz best quality vodka

3 drops Tabasco sauce

1tsp horseradish

8oz tomato juice, chilled

¼ tsp celery salt

⅛ tsp black pepper

1. Mix both the kosher and celery salt in a shallow dish.
2. Rub the rim of the glass with a wedge of lemon, and dip the glass into the salt dish so it clings to the rim.
3. Fill glass with ice.
4. Add Vodka, lemon juice, Worcestershire sauce, and Tobacco sauce.
5. Stir in the tomato juice with long spoon.
6. Add horseradish, sea salt, remaining celery salt, and pepper.
7. Stir again and serve with wedge of lemon.

# peach nectar bellini cocktail

1 part chilled peach nectar or white peach puree

1 part peach schnapps

4 parts Italian dry sparkling wine or dry champagne

1. Chill all ingredients ahead of time.
2. Pour the peach nectar and peach schnapps into the bottom of each fluted champagne glass with sparkling wine or dry champagne and serve.

# orange banana mimosa

Servings: 8 to 12

1 bottle of champagne

1 quart orange juice

grand marnier orange liquor to taste

½ banana, ripe

1. Pre-chill all ingredients.
2. Mash ripe banana in glass until almost a puree.
3. Fill each glass half full with ice
4. Add orange juice until the glass is ½ full.
5. Slowly pour in the champagne and stir.
6. Pour a splash of Grand Marnier Liquor on top.
7. Garnish with a slice of strawberry.
8. Serve these mimosas for breakfast or brunch.

# Boston cooler

1 lemon

1 tbsp grenadine

ginger ale to taste

1. Using citrus stripper or sharp fruit knives, peel the lemon so the skin forms a spiral.
2. Put the spiral, grenadine, and ice cubes into a highball glass.
3. Gently mix everything together with bar spoon.
4. Fill the glass with ginger ale and serve with thick straw.

# American lemonade

Servings: 2

½ tbsp sugar syrup

½ juice of lemon

1 slice of lemon

soda water to taste

1. Fill a highball glass half full with ice cubes.
2. Add lemon juice and sugar syrup.
3. Stir thoroughly with a bar spoon.
4. Fill the glass with soda water.
5. Garnish with the lemon slice, and serve with a straw.

# blushing virgin

Servings: 1

1 scoop vanilla ice cream

1 blood oranges juiced

5oz soda water, well chilled

1 orange peel

1. Put vanilla ice cream into a highball glass.

2. Add orange juice and fill the glass with soda water.

3. Drape the orange-peel spiral over the rim of the glass.

# strawberry margarita

Servings: 2

2 cups crushed ice

½ cup strawberry puree

1 cup tequila

2 limes, juiced

triple sec to taste

1 tbsp simple syrup

1. In a blender, combine ice, strawberry puree, tequila, lime juice, Triple Sec and simple syrup.

2. Puree until smooth.

3. Pour into rocks glasses and serve.

# miami vice

Servings: 2

2oz rum, divided

4oz pina colada mix

4oz strawberry daiquiri mix

3 cups crushed ice, divided

1. Blend 1oz rum, 1 ½ cups ice and pina colada mix for about 10 seconds, pour into a cup and set aside.

2. Rinse blender.

3. Combine 1oz rum, strawberry daiquiri mix and 1 ½ cup ice in the blender.

4. Blend for about 10 seconds.

5. Pour ingredients from blender and cup simultaneously into another cup.

6. You should have Pina Colada on one side and Strawberry Daiquiri on the other side.

# blackberry mojito

Servings: 2

¼ cup blackberries

2 tbsp simple syrup

1 tbsp lime juice

3oz white rum

3 mint leaves

cracked ice to taste

1. In a bar shaker, crush together blackberries, mint leaves, sugar and lime juice with a mortar or the back of a spoon until the mixture becomes slightly mushy.

2. Add rum and ice.

3. Shake and serve in Tom Collins.

4. Garnish with a lime slice

# mango mojito

Servings: 1

1 lime wedges

5 fresh mint leaves

¼ cup club soda

2 tbsp rum

3 tbsp simple syrup

1 tbsp mango nectar

crushed ice to taste

1. Squeeze the lime wedges into a small glass, add wedges and mint to glass. Crush with the back of a spoon for 30 seconds.

2. Add soda, rum, simple syrup, and nectar.

3. Stir gently.

4. Serve over ice.

# key lime pie

Servings: 1

½ lime, cut into wedges

4oz vodka

1 ½ oz frozen lemonade concentrate, thawed

1 tsp vanilla extract

2 twists lime zest, garnish

1. Place the lime wedges in the bottom of a glass and muddle them well.

2. Cover with ice, and pour in vodka, lime juice, and vanilla.

3. Shake well, and then strain into two stemmed cocktail glasses.

4. Garnish each with a twist of lime.

CPSIA information can be obtained
at www.ICGtesting.com
Printed in the USA
BVOW03s2102010317

477528BV00003B/10/P